BENTO FOR BEGINNERS

BENTO
for BEGINNERS

60 RECIPES FOR EASY BENTO BOX LUNCHES

CHIKA RAVITCH

PHOTOGRAPHY BY MARIJA VIDAL

ROCKRIDGE
PRESS

For general information on our other products and services or to obtain technical support, please contact our Customer Care Department within the United States at (866) 744-2665, or outside the United States at (510) 253-0500.

Rockridge Press publishes its books in a variety of electronic and print formats. Some content that appears in print may not be available in electronic books, and vice versa.

Interior and Cover Designer: Eric Pratt
Art Producer: Sue Bischofberger
Editor: Bridget Fitzgerald
Production Editor: Andrew Yackira

Photography © Marija Vidal, 2019

Cover: Japanese-Style Fried Chicken (page 32); Green Pea Rice (page 30); Marinated Radishes and Bell Peppers (page 75)

ISBN: Print 978-1-64611-135-0 | eBook 978-1-64611-136-7

R0

To my mother
(March 10, 1947–April 25, 1995)
for giving me limitless love.
To my husband, Frank, for depthless support
in every way.

CONTENTS

INTRODUCTION

What is bento? Simply put, it's a boxed lunch—but I consider it a treasure box packed with delicious, healthy, well-balanced foods, all in one container. Nowadays in Japan, bentos are available in many markets and convenience stores. But homemade bento is much tastier and healthier.

I learned bento making from my mother, who made bentos for my lunch when I was a student, and then I made them for myself once I started working. Lately, cutesy and Instagrammable bentos have also become popular. There's also a trend to make "character bentos" for kids—making food look like anime characters, such as Pikachu. These sorts of bentos are, indeed, adorable, but they can take a long time to make. One does not need to take hours to make a delicious bento. Bentos can be easy, fun, and delicious—even without the cartoon characters.

I grew up in Osaka. When my sister and I were little, my mother cooked every meal from scratch for our family. At that time grocery stores didn't carry many prepared foods, there weren't a lot of convenience stores, and eating out was expensive. More importantly, our parents and grandparents taught us that homemade food was healthy and delicious. (In fact, a study by Tohoku University showed that eating a Japanese diet from that time period brings down blood sugar and decreases bad cholesterol after only 4 weeks.)

When I was a child, I loved staying in the kitchen with my mother and grandmother. I often asked them how and why they did certain things, and they always answered my questions. Now that I'm the one in the kitchen, I have their methods in mind when I cook. I also learned a lot about nutrition from them—and then continued to learn more when I studied chemistry as a university student. I've included some of my mother's and grandmother's best recipes in this book.

In the chapters that follow, I will introduce you to delicious, healthy, easy-to-prepare Japanese bento ideas. I've been documenting recipes for years on my blog, *Your Home for Homemade Japanese Food (Japanese-food.org)*, on which I feature authentic Japanese recipes made with ingredients you can find at most grocery stores or Asian markets. There are bentos for vegans and vegetarians in this book, too. As a bonus, most Japanese food is gluten free, as long as you use gluten-free soy sauce.

The recipes in this book offer the maximum benefit of delicious, healthy Japanese food without requiring hours of work in the kitchen. I will also show you how to make some dishes ahead of time and how to store them so you don't need to wake up early in the morning just to make your lunch.

Whether you are trying bento for the first time, looking for new bento ideas, or feeling intimidated because you saw too many cutesy versions on social media, this book is for you! I hope you will enjoy making and eating these delicious and healthy lunches.

BENTO BASICS

New to making bentos? You may think it's a lot of work, but in reality, making a bento box lunch is not difficult at all. I will teach you easy recipes to help you make healthy, filling, delicious bentos. All the recipes in this book can be made using familiar ingredients from your grocery store. I will also teach you time-saving tricks to make your bento preparation free of stress and fuss. Additionally, the bentos in this book are quite healthy, because bentos themselves are well-balanced meals made of small portions. I hope this book will be a handy reference for years to come.

THE POWER OF BENTO

Bento is so much more than a great pack-and-go lunch. Bentos have many positive benefits, both mental and physical. According to the World Health Organization, as of 2018, Japan had the world's highest longevity rate; an important reason why people in Japan live longer is that they eat a filling yet healthy diet. Bentos can be part of that all-important healthy diet by providing a compact way to eat satisfying, well-balanced dishes, often using natural and seasonal ingredients.

HISTORY

More than a thousand years ago, during the Heian period in Japan, people were already making bento. Workers often brought rice balls and pickled vegetables to work for lunch. People learned that short-grain Japanese rice (often called Japonica rice today) still tasted very good even after it had cooled. This was the start of something amazing! Over time, eating bento at room temperature became a Japanese tradition. Even now, many Japanese people eat their bentos without heating them up.

Beginning about 450 years ago, fancy luxury bento became popular for tea ceremonies and cherry blossom-viewing parties. This sort of professionally prepared bento grew in popularity among wealthier people as economic growth increased. But many people still made delicious bento at home, and bento culture remained strong even as it diversified.

The basic rule of a traditional Japanese diet is *ichi-juu san-sai*. This means that a meal should consist of one bowl of cooked rice, one kind of soup, and three vegetable, fish, or meat side dishes. Most Japanese-style bentos are still made using a version of this rule, except most do not include soup.

Many Japanese people learned to prepare bento by watching their mothers make bento boxes every morning—so, although cooking rice or frying chicken in the morning before work may seem difficult or time-consuming, once you learn some useful tricks, it becomes second nature. Many Japanese people make bento boxes for themselves and their families every day.

BENTO BENEFITS

There are many unexpected benefits to making your own bento box lunches. Here are just a few of their best qualities:

Healthy food: A traditional bento is full of homemade food made from fresh ingredients. Most bento recipes are low in processed sugar and sodium, and they don't need preservatives because they can be stored by quick-freezing or refrigerating when needed (I will teach you how). Processed foods tend to contain a lot of sugar, sodium, and preservatives, which give manufacturers a cheap way to make food last longer and taste better. But, of course, too much sugar is unhealthy, and too much sodium can make us bloated and can raise blood pressure in people sensitive to sodium. Additionally, even many store-prepared foods are high in calories, especially when compared to homemade versions.

Saving money: Estimates show that many people, even those on a budget, spend $5 to $10 a day on lunch. Compare that to the average cost of a delicious and filling homemade Japanese bento— about $1.85 a day! This includes rice (or another starch), chicken or other main protein, and two vegetable side dishes. Bentos can save you a lot of money each month while contributing to overall good health and nourishing you with a delicious meal to look forward to each day.

Environmental benefits: When you buy prepared food, it usually comes in a plastic container. Homemade bentos are served in reusable, easy-to-wash containers, and the individual dishes can be stored in reusable containers or zip-top freezer bags.

Reduced food waste: Store-bought prepared foods that you take for lunch often come in big portions and might contain a wilted salad or too-salty side that isn't your favorite. You may throw out the extra, or the parts you don't like, without even thinking about it. In Japan we learn a "simple diet," which means not wasting food and not eating too much. This helps conserve resources and avoid lifestyle-related diseases caused by lack of portion control. Bento boxes can be the perfect solution for busy people because they contain the right amounts and flavors for you!

Time savings: In Japan, people usually eat their bentos at their desks, in a cafeteria, or on a bench near their offices or schools. Estimates show that those who bring bento for lunch have twice the time to eat it than others who go to a restaurant or buy a take-out lunch. A bento saves you the time of standing in line to buy a meal and gives you more time with friends and colleagues—or yourself.

FLAVOR OVER FAVOR

The bentos in this book are not the kind of excessively decorative bentos that can be found on social media nowadays—instead, these are practical lunches (most ingredients can be purchased at your local grocery store) that taste amazing and can even be eaten cold. Plus, I will give you tips on how to improve the storage life of your ingredients and dishes without using any preservatives. All you need to do is follow the steps, and the results will be delicious, well-balanced, hearty bento box lunches that will energize you for your work, studies, or wherever the afternoon takes you.

In this book I will teach you time-saving tricks wherever I can and offer many recipes that can be made in larger quantities ahead of time and stored using quick and easy methods. The reason I strongly advocate recipes that can be made ahead, or quickly in the morning, is that I have made bento on a daily basis for years, so I know that no one wants to cook from scratch when they need to get to work or school. Making a daily bento is a lifestyle choice that doesn't require sacrificing sleep or commute time.

BENTO FORMULAS

A traditional Japanese-style bento is 30 to 50 percent rice. The rest is split among a main protein and about two cooked vegetable side dishes, fruits, or raw vegetables.

According to an ancient Buddhist concept, it is preferable for a meal to include these five colors: green, red, yellow, white, and black (brown). When a meal has these colors, we believe we can have the good fortune of a healthy life.

Moreover, in Japanese cuisine, we judge a meal using the five senses: touch, taste, vision, smell, and sound. Visual appeal is deeply connected with taste. When a dish is colorful, people tend to feel it is tastier. Additionally, vegetables use their colors as a protection mechanism against harmful bacteria and insects. As a result, the color helps preserve important nutrients, such as polyphenol, anthocyanin, beta carotene, and so on— "eating the rainbow" ensures that you meet a good variety of your nutritional needs. Well-balanced food diminishes sugar cravings, because your body is satisfied with the necessary nutrition.

Keep in mind, too, that you can pack healthy fruits and raw vegetables, such as grape tomatoes, in a separate container from the main bento box so they can be kept apart if the bento will be heated.

A BENTO-READY KITCHEN

Because you pack a bento first thing in the morning and eat it 4 to 5 hours later, you need a few simple guidelines to keep your bento box food safe. Proper food storage and preparation are key. In this section, I will walk you through storage and safety tips as well as the basic ingredients and kitchen items you'll want to keep on hand.

CONTAINERS

I highly recommend a leak-proof, BPA-free, dishwasher-safe, microwave-safe plastic bento box that has three or four removable compartments. A box that holds 20 to 30 ounces is a common size for adult bentos; I especially like the 23-ounce, four-compartment container from Komax Biokips. The removable compartments enable you to separate each dish in the box to prevent flavors from combining, control portion size, remove some foods if not everything need reheating, and make the box easier to clean in the dishwasher. Simply put all the parts in the dishwasher at night to have them ready for packing the next morning. If you prefer not to run your dishwasher daily, you might want to get more than one container or handwash the bento box and let it air dry.

There are other choices besides plastic, such as glass, stainless steel, and even wooden bento boxes. Glass is microwave- and dishwasher-safe, but it is heavy and breaks easily. Stainless steel is lightweight but not microwave-safe. Wood is what traditional Japanese bento boxes were made of, and it is still popular today. It keeps cooked rice tasting good, absorbs excess moisture from foods to help keep them from spoiling, and looks beautiful on Instagram! However, wood bento boxes are expensive and difficult to handle. They must be handwashed immediately and dried really well. So, for many practical reasons, plastic bento boxes are best—even in Japan, they are the most popular choice.

STORAGE AND SAFETY

Traditionally, bentos have always been eaten cold, so there are a number of ancient tricks to ensure food safety. The bentos I will teach you to make in this book are delicious when eaten cold, but some can of course be heated in the microwave. Follow these four important rules to keep your bento safe:

1. **Completely cook meat, fish, and eggs before placing them in your bento.**

2. **Avoid including wet ingredients (juicy fruits, vegetables, or dishes with lots of sauce), if possible.** For example, avoid watermelon and pickles with brine, and be sure to dry all washed raw vegetables. Excess moisture causes food to spoil more quickly.

3. **Don't store cooked short-grain rice in the refrigerator because it will become very dry and hard.** Freezing is the best way to preserve the taste and texture of cooked rice; it also allows the rice to absorb moisture without growing bacteria. Then you can just microwave individual portions in the morning while packing your bento.

4. **To avoid bacteria growth, it is important to avoid moisture and warm temperatures (85°F to 105°F), so always put a lid on the bento *after* its ingredients cool to room temperature.** Putting the lid on the bento before the food cools causes the bento box to retain high temperatures and accumulate moisture, which can allow bacteria to grow. The best time to prepare bento is first thing in the morning so you can let it cool while you get ready for the day. Then, put the lid on your bento before leaving the house.

TROUBLESHOOTING

To avoid too much flavor melding, use a bento box with compartments, or use parchment paper, aluminum foil (unless you plan to microwave the bento), or muffin liners as dividers. Dividers help keep the foods in the bento from touching each other so each component keeps its distinct flavor.

Additionally, it is best not to use seasonings with strong aromas, such as garlic or cumin, in your bento recipes. One time when I was a kid, my mother put garlicky dumplings in my bento—and the smell spread all over the classroom, even though I had put the bento in my locker and wrapped it with a kitchen towel.

When you put food with a strong color in your plastic bento box, such as tomato sauce or ketchup, you might want to wipe out the inside of the bento box after eating or rinse it under running water. This helps keep the plastic from becoming stained.

KEEP IN MIND

A few other helpful tips for a safe bento kitchen:

- Always wash your hands before you pack your bento box.

- Season dishes slightly more than you would normally. Salt is effective in helping prevent harmful bacteria and keeping the dishes from spoiling. It also makes the dishes taste better when eaten cold.

- Add a vinegary dish to your bento. Vinegar has an antibacterial effect, so the vinegary dish helps keep the bento safe.

- The best way to store bento is with ice packs in a cooler bag and to keep it away from warm places. Or, even better, refrigerate your bento, if possible.

- Always check the smell of your food before you eat. If anything smells different than it should, play it safe and skip it.

TOOLS AND EQUIPMENT

You don't need many tools for making bento. A good container to use as a bento box (see page 7) is obviously essential, as are chopsticks or silverware for eating. And, as previously discussed, I strongly recommend getting a cooler bag and ice packs for food safety reasons. Here are some other helpful tools:

Freezer-, microwave-, and dishwasher-safe reusable freezer bags, reusable wrap, and glass food storage containers: These are very useful for storing and heating food, and they're also environmentally friendly. I like Pyrex glass food storage containers with lids, ExcelGadgets reusable silicone stretch lids for bowls, and MOICO reusable silicone food storage bags.

Skewers: I use these to corral small, round foods (such as grape tomatoes and meatballs) together in one place.

Rice cooker: Because all Japanese-style bentos include cooked rice, it is very convenient to have a rice cooker so the rice is cooked perfectly. However, if you don't have a rice cooker, I will teach you an easy way to cook rice on the stovetop (see page 134).

EASY EXTRAS

If you stock a variety of options in your refrigerator or pantry, you can make your bento box even more mouthwatering and healthy. Here are some ideas:

Fruits and vegetables with low water content: apples, baby cucumbers, bananas, berries, cantaloupe, celery, cherries, grapes, kiwis, mandarin oranges, radishes, small tomatoes, and strawberries (wash and dry completely before packing)

Protein: cheese sticks, hardboiled eggs

Snacks: dried fruits, nuts

Dried fruits and nuts are perfect ingredients for bento because they don't add moisture, they're shelf stable at room temperature, they're nutritious, and they last a long time. Homemade vegetable chips are also great as a go-to snack. I prefer to avoid store-bought vegetable chips because they tend to contain a lot of sodium.

Add any of these easy extras to your bento. For example, I keep cheese sticks and grape tomatoes on hand to fill my bento when it needs one more ingredient. I add skewered tomatoes and cut cheese, which make the bento more colorful, filling, and delicious. (Plus, in Japan, red and white is a lucky color combination.)

In Japan, we don't usually pack sweet desserts for school or the office, so Japanese-style bentos have vegetables or fruits as easy extras. However, in the Western-style bento and fusion bento recipes in this book, you'll find a few treats, such as muffins and chocolate fudge.

INGREDIENTS

Before we start cooking, let's talk about some main ingredients and seasonings, plus other things you might want to keep on hand.

Fresh Fruits

- Apples
- Grapes
- Melons

Fresh Vegetables

- Baby cucumbers
- Broccoli
- Carrots
- Ginger
- Grape tomatoes
- Scallions

Frozen Fruits and Vegetables

- Asparagus
- Blueberries
- Edamame
- Green peas
- Sweet corn

Proteins

- Eggs
- Cheese sticks
- Ham or bacon
- Tofu

Grains

- Dried penne or spaghetti
- Uncooked rice

Seeds and Nuts

- Roasted sesame seeds
- Walnuts

Seasonings

- Cooking sake
- Mirin (sweet cooking rice wine, available at many grocery stores and Asian markets, or on Amazon)
- Mixed (awase) miso paste (available at many Asian markets or on Amazon)
- Rice vinegar
- Soy sauce
- Toasted sesame oil
- Dashi: I sometimes make dashi stock from scratch, which is good for soup dishes, but dashi stock powder is better for bento safety. Dashi powder also lasts longer, flavors dishes, and can be used in any recipe, including scrambled eggs, without making the dish too moist. You can use any of the following brands, available at Asian markets or on Amazon:
  - Ajinomoto Hondashi bonito soup stock powder and consommé powder
  - Kayanoya Original dashi stock powder and vegetable stock powder
  - Shimaya kombu dashi seaweed soup stock powder

The beauty of using many of these fresh ingredients is that in addition to being delicious, they are nutritious. However, some vegetables and fruits are perishable, so I prefer not to store them long term, and I tend to go to the market to get fresh ingredients twice a week. To plan ahead for when I have no time to grocery shop, I always keep frozen packages of perishable foods on hand, or I buy fresh and prepare recipes in large batches, then refrigerate or freeze the food in individual portions.

PREPPING & ORGANIZING

Making bento is very simple when you follow the directions in this book and use the prep times at the top of each recipe to help you plan efficiently. Here is a step-by-step guide to making and packing your weekly lunches.

1. Look through the recipes in this book and note which bentos you want to bring for lunch over the next week. This is the fun part!

2. Make a shopping list of any items you don't have on hand, then head to the grocery store.

3. Cook and store your dishes when you have time, such as a few days before you plan to eat them. Most of the recipes in this book are not overly complicated and can be made a few days ahead to refrigerate or freeze.

4. Each morning, prep and pack your lunch for the day. Some dishes are best cooked in the morning, but these take only 5 to 10 minutes. Make your lunch while you drink your morning coffee or tea.

As you've already learned, most bentos consist of one carb dish (such as rice or pasta), one protein dish (such as chicken or tofu), one cooked vegetable dish (such as potato salad or sautéed sweet corn), and some easy extras. So, to prep for your weekly bento plan, you'll need at least one carb dish stored and ready to go, and it's great to have two or three cooked protein dishes and vegetable dishes in the freezer or refrigerator. How many dishes you make ahead and store depends on your plans for the week. If you pick just one bento and bring the same one every day, you can, theoretically, prepare one carb, one protein, and one vegetable dish for a week's worth of bentos.

A helpful organizing tip is to put a label on each storage container with the dish category (protein, carb, or vegetable) and the date you made it, then group the containers by labels in the freezer or refrigerator.

HOW TO USE THIS BOOK

The recipes in this book are broken into three sections: traditional Japanese bento boxes; Western-style bento boxes, which include American comfort foods with a bento approach; and fusion-style bento boxes, featuring tasty combinations of both Japanese and non-Japanese foods. Choose recipes from any of these bento styles based on your preferences.

These recipes can, for the most part, be made ahead and refrigerated for up to five days or frozen for about three weeks. Dishes that must be cooked in the morning can be prepared in less than 10 minutes. Moreover, there are some vegan, vegetarian, and gluten-free recipes included, and I suggest substitutions where relevant so everyone can use this book, whether you are a meat eater, pescatarian, vegetarian, or vegan.

There are no strict rules about how to pack a bento box, so it is fine to change up the combination of recipes—if, for instance, you find you don't have an ingredient stocked or you just want to try mixing and matching. All the bentos in this book offer filling—but healthy—portion sizes and are packed with nutrition for an energizing and convenient lunch on the go.

Let's get cooking!

2

JAPANESE-STYLE BENTOS

This chapter will teach you how to make authentic Japanese bentos using traditional recipes. These bentos contain delicious, nutritious, well-balanced, and beautiful components. *Washoku* (traditional Japanese cuisine) highlights colorful, fresh ingredients based on the four seasons and focuses on five tastes: sweet, sour, salty, bitter, and umami.

There are many authentic Japanese cookbooks out there, but it can be difficult to find the ingredients you need unless you live in Japan or have a really excellent Asian market available to you. This is why I started my blog and am writing this book. I will show you how to make traditional Japanese bentos—but with ingredients available at your local grocery store.

CHICKEN TERIYAKI BENTO

Chicken teriyaki is one of the most famous Japanese dishes in the world. It is both an essential dish for everyday life in Japan and a component of fancy store-bought bentos. I put the chicken teriyaki together with buttery corn rice (which kids love) and broccoli with sesame sauce. This bento contains healthy carbs and fat, plenty of protein, and lots of vitamins. I recommend adding easy extras that are high in minerals to round out the nutritional benefits of the other ingredients.

TIMING & PREP

Corn Rice (page 21): Make ahead (75 minutes) and freeze for up to 3 weeks.

Chicken Teriyaki (page 23): Make ahead (20 minutes) and refrigerate for up to 5 days.

Broccoli with Sesame Dressing (page 24): Make ahead (10 minutes) and refrigerate for up to 3 days.

In the morning: Microwave one serving of rice, covered, for 2 to 3 minutes. Microwave 1 piece of chicken, covered, for 30 seconds, then slice it. Pack the rice and chicken with one serving of cold broccoli in a bento box.

Easy extra suggestions: banana, berries, cheese stick, mandarin orange, nuts

CORN RICE

Up until the postwar era in Japan, people used to eat multigrain rice, a combination of sprouted brown rice, quinoa, millet, corn, barley, red rice, and other grains. Then, during a period of high economic growth, eating white rice became more mainstream. Lately, multigrain rice has regained popularity because of its health benefits. Sweet corn makes white rice more nutritious and is also good for kids, since the fresh kernels give the rice a slightly buttery taste. If you don't like plain white rice, combine the corn with another grain.

STORAGE: Up to 3 weeks in the freezer

PREP TIME: 40 min
COOK TIME: 35 min

1½ cups uncooked short-grain white rice

1⅔ cups water

Kernels from 1 ear fresh corn

1 tablespoon butter or margarine

MAKE AHEAD

1. In a fine-mesh strainer set atop a bowl, rinse the rice under cool running water while stirring it with your hand. Drain the rice as soon as the water in the bowl turns a murky white color. Repeat until the water in the bowl is clear.

2. In a medium bowl, combine the rice and water; let soak for 30 minutes at room temperature.

3. Pour the rice with the soaking water into a deep saucepan and add the corn. Cover the pan and bring the mixture to a boil over high heat, about 5 minutes. Turn the heat to very low and cook for 10 to 12 minutes. When there is no water left in the pan, turn off the heat, put a kitchen towel under the lid, and steam the rice and corn for 10 minutes. This makes the rice softer. Stir in the butter.

continued

4. Divide the rice into four portions, and transfer each portion to a zip-top bag or glass container.

IN THE MORNING

Microwave one portion of the frozen rice, covered, for 2 to 3 minutes, then transfer to the bento box.

Cooking tip: Before putting a kitchen towel over the rice, check inside the pan. If there is still water in the pan, put the lid back on and cook for 2 more minutes, then check again.

Ingredient tip: If you use unsalted butter, add 1 teaspoon salt when you cook the rice.

Substitution tip: For convenience, you can use ½ cup of frozen corn kernels. Add them to the pan once the rice and water come to a boil.

Per serving: Calories: 327; Total fat: 4g; Sodium: 40mg; Cholesterol: 0mg; Total carbs: 67g; Fiber: 3g; Sugar: 1g; Protein: 6g

CHICKEN TERIYAKI

In my (humble) opinion, teriyaki dishes outside of Japan are slightly different than Japanese teriyaki—they're usually way too sweet. Here, I want you to taste authentic teriyaki, which is delicious and not greasy. The keys to perfect chicken are panfrying and pan-steaming. These methods make the chicken soft, juicy, and perfectly moist in a short amount of cooking time. You can cook this dish the night before and refrigerate it, though it's quick and easy enough to whip up in the morning.

STORAGE: Up to 5 days in the refrigerator

PREP TIME: 5 min
COOK TIME: 15 min

1 tablespoon
vegetable oil

4 boneless, skinless
chicken thighs

1 tablespoon
cooking sake

¼ cup Versatile Sauce
(page 136)

1 teaspoon grated
peeled fresh ginger

THE NIGHT BEFORE

1. In a skillet, heat the vegetable oil over medium heat until it shimmers. Add the chicken and cook for 4 minutes. Flip the chicken, add the cooking sake, cover the skillet, and reduce the heat to low. Steam the chicken for 3 minutes.

2. Add the Versatile Sauce and ginger. Increase the heat to medium and simmer for 6 minutes, turning the chicken occasionally and using a spoon to baste it with the sauce frequently, until the sauce is almost completely reduced.

3. Transfer the chicken to a clean container to cool, then cover and refrigerate.

IN THE MORNING

Microwave 1 chicken thigh, covered, for 30 seconds, cut it into slices, and add to the bento box.

Substitution tip: If you prefer, use any kind of broth instead of cooking sake to steam the chicken.

Per serving: Calories: 192; Total fat: 8g; Sodium: 610mg; Cholesterol: 95mg; Total carbs: 6g; Fiber: 0g; Sugar: 4g; Protein: 22g

BROCCOLI WITH SESAME DRESSING

I was so surprised the first time I saw people eating raw broccoli in Canada 20 years ago. In Japan, broccoli is never eaten raw because it is hard to digest. Cooked vegetables have a smaller volume than raw vegetables, so we can eat more and get more nutritional benefits. Still, overcooking broccoli breaks down its vitamin C content. We have to choose the correct cooking method based on each vegetable's characteristics.

STORAGE: Up to 3 days in the refrigerator

PREP TIME: 5 min
COOK TIME: 5 min

1 teaspoon salt

1 large head broccoli, cut into small florets, stems peeled and sliced

⅓ cup Sesame Dressing (page 137)

THE NIGHT BEFORE

1. Fill a large bowl with ice-cold water and set aside.

2. Fill a large saucepan with water and add the salt. Bring it to a boil over high heat, add the broccoli, and cook for 3 minutes. Transfer the broccoli to the cold water and let sit for about 2 minutes to stop the cooking process. Drain and transfer to paper towels. Gently blot the broccoli dry with more paper towels.

3. Transfer the broccoli to a medium bowl and add the dressing. Gently toss to coat. Transfer the dressed broccoli to a clean container, cover, and refrigerate.

IN THE MORNING

Put one-third of the cold broccoli in the bento box.

Safety tip: In the refrigerator, the dressed broccoli will give off some water because of the salt content in the soy sauce. Transfer just the broccoli to your bento box, leaving the excess liquid behind.

Per serving: Calories: 136; Total fat: 7g; Sodium: 775mg; Cholesterol: 0mg; Total carbs: 18g; Fiber: 2g; Sugar: 12g; Protein: 3g

MISO-MARINATED SALMON BENTO

This sumptuous bento combines rice with flavorful chicken crumbles, miso-marinated grilled salmon, and homemade cucumber pickles. And the best part? This bento takes only 10 minutes to prepare. Packed with energizing nutrients from the chicken, salmon, miso, and ginger, it is a smart choice for a tough, busy day. You can prepare all the components the night before, or, if it's more convenient, cook the chicken crumbles a day or two ahead. For a beautiful presentation, add yellow or orange fruits as easy extras.

TIMING & PREP

Ginger Chicken Rice (page 26): Make the ginger chicken crumbles (25 minutes) and refrigerate for up to 4 days.

Miso-Marinated Grilled Salmon (page 27): Marinate the salmon in the miso sauce (10 minutes prep time) and refrigerate for up to 3 days.

Cucumber and Ginger Pickles (page 28): Make ahead (10 minutes) and refrigerate for up to 3 days.

In the morning: Cook the marinated salmon (10 minutes). Meanwhile, microwave one serving of frozen Steamed Rice (page 134), covered, for 2 to 3 minutes, put it in a bento box, and top with the cold chicken crumbles. Then, add the salmon and cold pickles to the bento box.

Easy extra suggestions: banana, cantaloupe, mandarin oranges

GINGER CHICKEN RICE

Ginger chicken crumbles are a common rice seasoning in Japan. They have a flavor-packed sweet and savory taste. Use them to top any dish you'd like, such as salad, pasta, pizza, or sautéed vegetables. Moreover, because of the simplicity of this recipe, you can add any spices to make the dish more flavorful. I sometimes add red pepper flakes or curry powder. When you have the chicken crumbles ready to go in your refrigerator, your options are endless.

STORAGE: Up to 4 days in the refrigerator

PREP TIME: 15 min
COOK TIME: 10 min

1 pound
ground chicken

½ cup Versatile Sauce
(page 136)

2 teaspoon grated
peeled fresh ginger

1 serving frozen
Steamed Rice
(page 134) per bento

THE DAY BEFORE

1. In a dry skillet, cook the ground chicken over medium heat, breaking it up with a spoon, until it is browned and no longer pink, about 5 minutes. Drain the excess fat.

2. Add the Versatile Sauce and ginger. Cook, stirring, until the sauce is reduced, about 5 minutes.

3. Let cool before transferring the chicken crumbles to a clean container to refrigerate.

IN THE MORNING

Microwave the frozen rice, covered, for 2 to 3 minutes. Add it to the bento box and top with one-fourth of the chicken crumbles.

Per serving: Calories: 278; Total fat: 9g; Sodium: 1094mg; Cholesterol: 96mg; Total carbs: 26g; Fiber: 0g; Sugar: 8g; Protein: 22g

MISO-MARINATED GRILLED SALMON

This dish will give you a fresh perspective on miso and salmon. Many restaurants have a similar dish, but this homemade version is incredibly delicious and easy to cook. The best part is that the salmon is cooked in a parchment paper–lined pan for easy cleanup. Miso (soybean paste) is a traditional Japanese fermented food product. It contains probiotics and healthy bacteria, and the Japanese believe it helps keep the doctor away.

STORAGE: Up to 3 days in the refrigerator

PREP TIME: 10 min
COOK TIME: 10 min

3 tablespoons mixed (awase) miso

2 tablespoons cooking sake

2 tablespoons mirin

1 (5- to 6-ounce) skinless salmon fillet, cut into 1-inch pieces

THE NIGHT BEFORE

In a small bowl, whisk together the miso, cooking sake, and mirin. Transfer the marinade to a large zip-top bag. Add the salmon to the marinade, seal the bag, and turn the salmon so it is completely covered with the sauce. Refrigerate overnight or for up to 3 days.

IN THE MORNING

1. Remove half of the salmon and wipe off the excess marinade using paper towels.

2. Line a skillet with parchment paper and put it over medium-low heat. Add the salmon and cook for 4 minutes. Flip the salmon and reduce the heat to low. Cover the skillet and cook for 5 minutes more.

3. Transfer the cooked salmon to the bento box.

Cooking tip: Miso sauce can burn easily, so don't skip lining the skillet with the parchment. As you cook the salmon, remove the excess sauce.

Per serving: Calories: 225; Total fat: 8g; Sodium: 1594mg; Cholesterol: 0mg; Total carbs: 15g; Fiber: 2g; Sugar: 6g; Protein: 23g

CUCUMBER AND GINGER PICKLES

This is a quick and easy pickle recipe. It doesn't take a lot of time to marinate because the irregular surfaces quickly absorb the pickling liquid. Fresh ginger adds wonderful health benefits, such as helping blood flow, increasing metabolism, and blocking the oxidation process in our bodies. It also has antibacterial properties—this is why sushi is served with ginger.

 STORAGE: Up to 3 days in the refrigerator

 **PREP TIME:** 10 min

4 baby cucumbers, trimmed

¼ cup Pickling Liquid (page 138)

1 teaspoon grated peeled fresh ginger

¼ teaspoon salt

Roasted sesame seeds, for garnish

THE NIGHT BEFORE

1. Wrap each cucumber with a kitchen towel and smash it with a rolling pin until it breaks into about ½-inch pieces. Use your fingers to adjust the pieces to the correct size.

2. In a medium bowl, stir together the pickling liquid, ginger, and salt. Add the cucumber and mix well. Cover and refrigerate overnight.

IN THE MORNING

Put one-third of the cucumbers in the bento box and sprinkle with roasted sesame seeds.

Cooking tip: You can cut the cucumber with a knife instead of using the rolling pin, but then the cucumbers will need longer to marinate.

Substitution tip: Use any kind of cucumber, but the sauce may become watery and the taste may become diluted during storage because other types of cucumbers contain more water than baby cucumbers do.

Per serving: Calories: 96; Total fat: 7g; Sodium: 422mg; Cholesterol: omg; Total carbs: 7g; Fiber: 1g; Sugar: 3g; Protein: 1g

FRIED CHICKEN BENTO

Japanese-style fried chicken is an essential food for bento. Everybody loves it. It is healthy and filling, and it's a great gluten-free option if you use gluten-free soy sauce. In this bento, I include green pea rice and pan-fried potato and carrot with the chicken. Authentic Japanese bentos rarely include raw vegetables as a side dish. They sometimes have small tomatoes or lettuce but only to fill a small gap or add color. Vegetables in Japanese bentos are always simmered, marinated, and/or sautéed. As this bento is already high in good carbs, add fruits and veggies that are low in carbs for your easy extras.

TIMING & PREP

Green Pea Rice (page 30): Make ahead (75 minutes) and freeze for up to 3 weeks.

Japanese-Style Fried Chicken (page 32): Make ahead (60 minutes) and freeze for up to 3 weeks.

Pan-Fried Potato and Carrot (page 35): Make ahead (15 minutes) and refrigerate for up to 4 days.

In the morning: Microwave one serving of rice, covered, for 2 to 3 minutes. Then, microwave 3 or 4 pieces of chicken, wrapped in paper towels, for 1 minute. Combine the rice and chicken with the cold pan-fried vegetables in a bento box.

Easy extra suggestions: berries, cantaloupe, kiwi (halved; bring a spoon), grape tomatoes

GREEN PEA RICE

This rice has a slightly salty flavor and a very tender texture. Green peas are high in protein, vitamins, and minerals, and have more vitamin B_1 and fiber than many other vegetables do. I use frozen peas because they are handy, but you can also use fresh peas. In that case, add the fresh peas to the pan when you begin to cook the rice.

STORAGE: Up to 3 weeks in the freezer

PREP TIME: 40 min
COOK TIME: 35 min

1½ cups uncooked short-grain white rice

1⅔ cups water

1½ teaspoons cooking sake

1 teaspoon salt

⅓ cup frozen green peas, rinsed to thaw

MAKE AHEAD

1. In a fine-mesh strainer set atop a bowl, rinse the rice under cool running water while stirring it with your hand. Drain the rice as soon as the water in the bowl turns a murky white color. Repeat until the water in the bowl is clear.

2. In a medium bowl, combine the rice and water; let soak for 30 minutes at room temperature.

3. Pour the rice with the soaking water into a deep saucepan and add the cooking sake and salt. Cover the pan and bring the mixture to a boil over high heat, about 5 minutes. Add the peas and gently stir. Turn the heat to very low, cover the pan, and cook for 10 to 12 minutes. When there is no water left in the pan, turn off the heat, put a kitchen towel under the lid, and steam the rice and peas for 10 minutes. This makes the rice softer. Stir carefully from the bottom of the pan.

4. Divide the rice into four portions, and transfer each portion to a zip-top bag or glass container.

IN THE MORNING

Microwave one portion of the frozen rice, covered, for 2 to 3 minutes, then transfer to the bento box.

Cooking tip: Before putting the kitchen towel over the rice to steam, check inside the pan. If there is still water in the pan, put the lid back on and cook for 2 more minutes, then check again. If you cook the rice in a rice cooker, add the peas at the beginning, since you cannot open the cooker while it is cooking.

Per serving: Calories: 279; Total fat: 0g; Sodium: 583mg; Cholesterol: 0mg; Total carbs: 61g; Fiber: 6g; Sugar: 1g; Protein: 6g

JAPANESE-STYLE FRIED CHICKEN

This is a popular dish called karaage in Japanese. It is fried marinated chicken thighs with soy sauce and ginger, and it is incredibly flavorful. The big differences between this dish and American fried chicken are that the batter is very thin and isn't seasoned and the chicken is served in bite-size pieces, which makes it very tender and juicy. Once you have a bite, you won't be able to stop eating it!

STORAGE: Up to 3 weeks in the freezer

PREP TIME: 25 min
COOK TIME: 35 min

3 pounds boneless, skinless chicken thighs (about 8 thighs), cut into 2-inch pieces

1 teaspoon grated peeled fresh ginger

2 tablespoons soy sauce (gluten free if necessary)

1 tablespoon cooking sake

¼ cup cornstarch

Vegetable oil, for frying

MAKE AHEAD

1. In a large bowl, combine the chicken, ginger, soy sauce, and cooking sake. Submerge the chicken into the sauce and refrigerate to marinate for 15 minutes.

2. Add the cornstarch and stir to coat the chicken completely.

3. Heat 1 inch of vegetable oil in a deep pan over medium heat until it shimmers. Fry 4 to 5 pieces of chicken at a time for 4 minutes, flipping occasionally, until golden brown. Transfer to paper towels to drain. Repeat with the remaining chicken.

4. Let cool before transferring to a zip-top bag to freeze.

IN THE MORNING

Wrap 3 or 4 pieces of chicken in a paper towel and microwave for 1 minute. Transfer the chicken to the bento box.

Cleanup tip: Do not drain the used oil down the sink. Instead, stuff some used paper towels into an empty can or jar and pour the cooled oil into the container so it is absorbed. Throw out the can or jar as regular garbage.

Cooking tip: To check that the oil is hot enough for frying, drop in some batter. If it floats with bubbles, the oil is ready.

Safety tip: To fry the chicken safely, use a deep pan with sides at least three times the height of the amount of oil used. While frying, put a metal strainer upside-down, like a lid, over the pan. This prevents oil from spattering everywhere.

Per serving: Calories: 347; Total fat: 16g; Sodium: 501mg; Cholesterol: 190mg; Total carbs: 5g; Fiber: 0g; Sugar: 0g; Protein: 44g

PAN-FRIED POTATO AND CARROT

This dish, a traditional Japanese side dish called kinpira, *is popular with foreigners who read my blog. It has a sweet-savory flavor, and the vegetables have a crunchy texture. In Japan we usually use gobo (burdock root), but I can't find that easily at my local grocery store, so I use potato and carrot. It turns out just as delicious.*

STORAGE: Up to 4 days in the refrigerator

PREP TIME: 5 min
COOK TIME: 10 min

1 tablespoon toasted sesame oil

1 large russet potato, peeled and cut into thin 2-inch strips

1 carrot, cut into thin 2-inch strips

¼ cup Versatile Sauce (page 136)

1 tablespoon soy sauce (gluten free if necessary)

1 teaspoon Shimaya kombu dashi soup stock powder, or any vegetable- or fish-based dashi powder

1½ teaspoons roasted sesame seeds

THE NIGHT BEFORE

1. In a skillet, heat the sesame oil over medium heat until it shimmers. Add the potato and carrot and cook until they are coated with the oil. Add the Versatile Sauce, soy sauce, and dashi powder. Stir-fry for 8 minutes.

2. Let cool before transferring to a clean container to refrigerate.

IN THE MORNING

Put one-fourth of the cold vegetables in the bento box, and sprinkle with roasted sesame seeds.

Variation tip: If you don't follow a vegetarian diet, add thinly sliced pork or small pieces of boneless chicken. Also, the dish can be made spicy using red pepper flakes, if you'd like.

Per serving: Calories: 143; Total fat: 4g; Sodium: 751mg; Cholesterol: 0mg; Total carbs: 25g; Fiber: 2g; Sugar: 5g; Protein: 3g

MUSHROOM RICE BENTO

I love to eat this classic bento when I have less of an appetite, like on a hot, humid summer day, because it contains light, easy-to-digest foods. All the components are great for vegetarians and can be gluten free if you use gluten-free soy sauce. Plus, most of the recipes can be prepared ahead. The only thing you need to cook in the morning is the egg, which takes less than 5 minutes. For a beautiful presentation, add red fruits or veggies.

TIMING & PREP

Mushroom Rice (page 37): Make ahead (75 minutes) and freeze for up to 3 weeks.

Green Beans with Sesame Dressing (page 39): Make ahead (15 minutes) and refrigerate for up to 3 days.

Microwaved Fried Egg (page 40): Cook in the morning (4 minutes).

In the morning: Microwave one serving of rice, covered, for 2 to 3 minutes. Then, cook the egg in the microwave (4 minutes). Combine the rice and egg with the cold green beans in a bento box.

Easy extra suggestions: cherries, grape tomatoes, radishes, red grapes, strawberries

MUSHROOM RICE

This is a very flavorful steamed, seasoned rice. We mostly use white rice in Japanese cooking, but sometimes we add other ingredients and seasonings to give it a variety of delicious flavors. Mushrooms are low in calories and high in fiber and minerals. Use any fresh mushrooms for this recipe; if you use dried shiitake mushrooms, the dish will be more nutritious and have a deeper umami flavor, because the dried version contains 30 times the nutrients of fresh shiitakes and has richer flavor. Soak the dried shiitakes overnight in the refrigerator, or microwave with some water for 3 minutes to reconstitute them before cooking.

STORAGE: Up to 3 weeks in the freezer

PREP TIME: 40 min
COOK TIME: 35 min

1½ cups uncooked short-grain white rice

1⅓ cups water

8 ounces cremini mushrooms or any mushrooms you like, stemmed and chopped

3 tablespoons soy sauce (gluten free if necessary)

1 tablespoon cooking sake

1 tablespoon mirin

1 teaspoon Shimaya kombu dashi soup stock powder or any vegetable- or fish-based dashi powder

½ teaspoon salt

MAKE AHEAD

1. In a fine-mesh strainer set atop a bowl, rinse the rice under cool running water while stirring it with your hand. Drain the rice as soon as the water in the bowl turns a murky white color. Repeat until the water in the bowl is clear.

2. In a medium bowl, combine the rice and water; let soak for 30 minutes at room temperature.

3. Pour the rice with the soaking water into a deep saucepan, and add the mushrooms, soy sauce, cooking sake, mirin, dashi powder, and salt. Cover the pan and bring the mixture to a boil over high heat, about 5 minutes. Turn the heat to very low and cook for 10 to 12 minutes. When there is no water left in the pan, turn off the heat, put a kitchen towel under the lid, and steam the rice and mushrooms for 10 minutes. This makes the rice softer. Stir carefully from the bottom of the pan.

continued

4. Divide the rice into four portions, and transfer each portion to a zip-top bag or glass container.

IN THE MORNING

Microwave one portion of the frozen rice, covered, for 2 to 3 minutes. Transfer the rice to the bento box.

Cooking tip: Before putting the kitchen towel over the rice to steam, check inside the pan. If there is still water in the pan, put the lid back on and cook for 2 more minutes, then check again.

Per serving: Calories: 297; Total fat: 0g; Sodium: 1000mg; Cholesterol: 0mg; Total carbs: 64g; Fiber: 3g; Sugar: 1g; Protein: 8g

GREEN BEANS WITH SESAME DRESSING

This traditional side dish is called goma-ae in Japanese. Boiled green beans are dressed with a slightly sweet sesame dressing. I use fresh green beans, but frozen green beans will work, too. I usually buy lots of fresh green beans when they look good, wash and dry them, and freeze them. The beauty of using frozen vegetables is that there is no need to add oil when cooking because the moisture from the frozen vegetables steams them in the pan.

STORAGE: Up to 3 days in the refrigerator

PREP TIME: 5 min
COOK TIME: 10 min

1 tablespoon salt

12 ounces (about 2¼ cups) fresh green beans, trimmed and cut into 2-inch pieces

¼ cup Sesame Dressing (page 137)

THE NIGHT BEFORE

1. Fill a large bowl with ice-cold water and set aside.

2. Fill a large saucepan with water and add the salt. Bring it to a boil over high heat, add the green beans, and reduce the heat to medium. Cook the green beans for 5 minutes, then transfer them to the cold water and let sit for 2 minutes to stop the cooking. Drain and put the beans on paper towels; blot dry.

3. Transfer the dried green beans to a large bowl, add the sesame dressing, and gently toss to coat. Put the dressed green beans in a clean container, cover, and refrigerate.

IN THE MORNING

Put one-third of the cold green beans in the bento box.

Per serving: Calories: 103; Total fat: 4g; Sodium: 781mg; Cholesterol: 0mg; Total carbs: 17g; Fiber: 5g; Sugar: 5g; Protein: 4g

MICROWAVED FRIED EGG

We usually use a special rectangular pan for this recipe, but I will teach you how to cook it in the microwave in less than 2 minutes. It doesn't have the same shape as traditional Japanese pan-fried eggs, but it is still delicious. In Japan, this kind of fried egg is very popular. People like it more than scrambled or sunny-side up eggs. We put this dish in our bento almost every day and frequently add it to our meals as a side dish.

PREP TIME: 2 min
COOK TIME: 2 min

2 large eggs

1½ teaspoons sugar

½ teaspoon rice vinegar

IN THE MORNING

1. In a microwave-safe bowl, whisk together the eggs, sugar, and vinegar. Microwave for 40 seconds, then stir. Microwave for 40 seconds more. If there is still uncooked egg, cook for 10 seconds longer and check again.

2. When cooked through, fold the egg twice (or cut and stack it) to fit in the bento box.

Cleanup tip: After cooking the eggs in the microwave, the bowl may have a bit of egg caked on it. If you don't have time to clean it in the morning, sprinkle some baking soda in it, fill the bowl with water, and let it soak in the sink. When you have time later, it will wash easily.

Ingredient tip: Adding rice vinegar keeps the egg's color yellow but does not change the taste. (Microwaving sometimes changes an egg's color to purplish-blue because of the egg's chemical structure. This is natural and doesn't harm you.)

Per serving: Calories: 167; Total fat: 10g; Sodium: 140mg; Cholesterol: 372mg; Total carbs: 7g; Fiber: 0g; Sugar: 7g; Protein: 13g

TERIYAKI TOFU BENTO

This bento is delicious for everyone, especially vegans. It has protein from tofu and edamame and healthy fat from the sesame seeds. There is an old folk custom of eating soy products (beans), sesame seeds (nuts and seeds), seaweed, vegetables, fish, mushrooms, and potatoes on a daily basis in order to have a balanced diet. The Japanese learn to eat small amounts of these ingredients every day. Most dishes in this bento can be made ahead, but there is one recipe you cook in the morning—in just 10 minutes. For easy extras, add red fruits and veggies, which are high in vitamins.

TIMING & PREP

Sesame Seed Rice (page 42): Make the sesame seed rice seasoning ahead (2 minutes) and refrigerate for up to 1 month.
Teriyaki Tofu (page 43): Make ahead (25 minutes) and refrigerate for up to 4 days.
Sautéed Edamame and Corn (page 45): Cook in the morning (10 minutes).

In the morning: Cook the edamame and corn (10 minutes). Meanwhile, microwave one serving of frozen Steamed Rice (page 134), covered, for 2 to 3 minutes, then sprinkle with sesame seed seasoning. Microwave the tofu for 30 seconds. Combine the ingredients in a bento box.

Easy extra suggestions: berries, cherries, grape tomatoes, radishes, red grapes

SESAME SEED RICE

Japanese people eat rice every day in our bentos, but it is not always plain white rice. Sometimes we cook rice with other ingredients, pan-fry it, or use rice seasonings called furikake. There are many types of delicious furikake that are made with fish, Japanese basil, pickled plums, seaweed, and so on (many of which are available on Amazon or at your local Asian market). In this recipe I will teach you a traditional and easy-to-make rice seasoning: sesame seeds and salt. Sesame seeds are very nutritious. I recommend using roasted sesame seeds versus raw, because it is easier for us to absorb the nutrition from the roasted seeds.

STORAGE (SESAME SEED SEASONING): Up to 1 month in the refrigerator

PREP TIME: 2 min
COOK TIME: 3 min

1 tablespoon ground roasted sesame seeds

½ teaspoon fine sea salt

1 serving frozen Steamed Rice (page 134)

MAKE AHEAD

In a clean container with a lid, stir together the sesame seeds and salt. Cover and keep refrigerated.

IN THE MORNING

Microwave the frozen rice, covered, for 2 to 3 minutes. Transfer the rice to the bento box and sprinkle with about 1 teaspoon of the sesame seed seasoning.

Cooking tip: To grind sesame seeds, use a Japanese mortar and pestle or a clean spice grinder. If you don't have either, put the sesame seeds in a zip-top bag and crush them with a rolling pin.

Per serving: Calories: 150; Total fat: 5g; Sodium: 1mg; Cholesterol: 0mg; Total carbs: 20g; Fiber: 1g; Sugar: 0g; Protein: 2g

TERIYAKI TOFU

Nowadays, there are a lot of prepared teriyaki sauces on the market. My homemade teri-yaki sauce, which I call Versatile Sauce, has a delicious taste and is very easy to make. You can cook anything you want with this sauce, such as chicken, fish, or vegetables. Here, it makes the best Teriyaki Tofu—once you taste it, you won't want to buy the store-bought version ever again.

STORAGE: Up to 4 days in the refrigerator

PREP TIME: 15 min
COOK TIME: 10 min

1 (14-ounce) package extra-firm tofu

½ cup cornstarch

2 tablespoons toasted sesame oil

½ cup Versatile Sauce (page 136)

Chopped scallion, for garnish

THE NIGHT BEFORE

1. Drain the tofu and wrap it in paper towels, then put it on a microwave-safe plate. Microwave for 3 minutes. Change the paper towels if they are completely soaked, then put a weight, such as a heavy plate, on the wrapped tofu for at least 10 minutes to drain completely.

2. Cut the drained tofu into ½-inch cubes. Put the cornstarch in a shallow bowl. Dredge the tofu in the cornstarch and tap off any excess.

3. In a skillet, heat the sesame oil over medium heat until it shimmers. Add the tofu and cook for 7 minutes, flipping occasionally, until golden on all sides.

4. Add in the Versatile Sauce. Cook, stirring, for 2 minutes, or until the sauce is slightly thickened.

5. Let cool before transferring to a clean container to refrigerate.

continued

TERIYAKI TOFU continued

IN THE MORNING

Microwave one-third of the tofu for 30 seconds and put it in the bento box. Sprinkle with chopped scallion.

Storage tip: It is very handy to keep frozen chopped scallion in the freezer. You can use it without thawing. Wash the scallions, dry them well with paper towels, and finely chop them. Put them in a zip-top bag and freeze for up to 3 weeks.

Per serving: Calories: 332; Total fat: 17g; Sodium: 1038mg; Cholesterol: 0mg; Total carbs: 33g; Fiber: 1g; Sugar: 8g; Protein: 14g

SAUTÉED EDAMAME AND CORN

Edamame is a very nutritious and versatile ingredient. It is high in vitamins, protein, fiber, iron, and potassium. Enjoy it on its own, or add it to omelets, soup, salad, rice, pasta, and so on. In Japan, it's common as an appetizer with beer. I usually stock frozen shelled edamame in the freezer so I can cook healthy and delicious dishes in a short amount of time.

PREP TIME: 5 min
COOK TIME: 5 min

¼ cup frozen shelled edamame

¼ cup frozen corn kernels

Pinch salt

Pinch freshly ground black pepper

IN THE MORNING

In a dry saucepan, cook the edamame and corn over medium heat for 2 minutes. Season with salt and pepper and cook for 3 minutes more. Transfer the vegetables to the bento box.

Per serving: Calories: 58; Total fat: 1g; Sodium: 162mg; Cholesterol: 0mg; Total carbs: 10g; Fiber: 2g; Sugar: 2g; Protein: 3g

BAKED TOFU SPRING ROLL BENTO

This is one of my favorite bentos. It has great nutritional balance because of the salmon, beans, tofu, and cooked vegetables. This bento is a good choice for people who might need some convincing when it comes to fish, because the flaked salmon texture and taste are amazing. Also, I chop the vegetables into very small pieces for the spring rolls, so picky eaters cannot always tell exactly what is in there. In fact, I have a friend who claims she doesn't like mushrooms, but she loves these spring rolls.

TIMING & PREP

Rice with Flaked Salmon (page 47): Make the flaked salmon ahead (17 minutes) and refrigerate for up to 5 days.

Baked Tofu Spring Rolls (page 49): Make ahead (55 minutes) and freeze for up to 3 weeks.

Gomoku-Mame (Simmered Beans, page 51): Make ahead (40 minutes) and refrigerate for up to 5 days.

In the morning: Microwave the frozen Steamed Rice (page 134), covered, for 2 to 3 minutes, and mix with the flaked salmon. Microwave 2 spring rolls, covered, for 2 minutes. Combine the rice and spring rolls with the cold simmered beans in a bento box.

Easy extra suggestions: banana, cantaloupe, green grapes, kiwi (halved; bring a spoon)

RICE WITH FLAKED SALMON

Flaked salmon is a very popular rice seasoning in Japan, like ginger chicken crumbles (see Ginger Chicken Rice, page 26). This dish has a fluffy texture, slightly salty taste, and pronounced sesame oil flavor. Because the salmon is flaked, it doesn't have a strong fishy flavor or aroma. It is perfect to sprinkle on rice, salad, or pasta to add extra protein to your meal. In Japan we can get store-bought flaked salmon, but I prefer to make it myself because it tastes better.

STORAGE: Up to 5 days in the refrigerator

PREP TIME: 5 min
COOK TIME: 12 min

1 (5- to 6-ounce) salmon fillet

1 tablespoon toasted sesame oil

½ teaspoon salt

1 serving frozen Steamed Rice (page 134)

THE NIGHT BEFORE

1. Fill a medium saucepan with water, and bring it to a boil over high heat. Reduce the heat to medium, add the salmon, and boil for 5 minutes. Drain.

2. Using two forks, shred the cooked salmon, removing any skin and bones.

3. In a skillet, heat the sesame oil over medium heat until it shimmers. Add the shredded salmon and cook for 2 to 3 minutes, seasoning with the salt halfway through the cooking time.

4. Let cool before transferring to a clean container to refrigerate.

continued

IN THE MORNING

Microwave the frozen rice, covered, for 2 to 3 minutes.
Add one-third of the salmon and stir to combine.
Transfer the rice to a bento box.

Cooking tip: Overcooked salmon can be dry and tough, so avoid overcooking it. It is OK if the salmon isn't quite cooked through when you shred it because it will cook the rest of the way during the panfrying.

Per serving: Calories: 217; Total fat: 9g; Sodium: 613mg; Cholesterol: 0mg; Total carbs: 20g; Fiber: 1g; Sugar: 0g; Protein: 15g

BAKED TOFU SPRING ROLLS

These spring rolls contain tofu, carrots, and mushrooms as the main ingredients, and they are baked rather than fried, which makes this a fuss-free, healthy dish. The finished rolls have a crunchy outside and smooth and flavorful filling. They are irresistible. Learning to wrap spring rolls is not difficult—you will already be a pro when you roll your second one. If you have kids, it is fun to have them help.

 STORAGE: Up to 3 weeks in the freezer

 PREP TIME: 30 min
COOK TIME: 25 min

Nonstick cooking spray

1 (14-ounce) package firm or extra-firm tofu

4 cremini mushrooms (or any mushrooms you like), stemmed and finely chopped

1 carrot, finely chopped

1 teaspoon grated peeled fresh ginger

1 teaspoon salt

1 teaspoon soy sauce

1 large egg, beaten

20 spring roll wrappers

1 tablespoon vegetable oil

MAKE AHEAD

1. Preheat the oven to 400°F. Coat a rimmed baking sheet with cooking spray and set aside.

2. Drain the tofu and wrap it in paper towels, then put it on a microwave-safe plate. Microwave for 3 minutes. Before microwaving, change the paper towels if they are completely soaked.

3. In a large bowl, combine the mushrooms, carrot, ginger, salt, soy sauce, and egg.

4. Using your hands, crumble the tofu into the bowl, as finely as you can, and mix it well with the other ingredients.

continued

5. Put a spring roll wrapper on a dry work surface with a point facing you. Place 1 heaping tablespoon of the tofu mixture on the wrapper toward the bottom center. Fold the bottom of the wrapper over the filling. Fold the right side of the wrapper to the center. Roll the wrapper away from you. Fold the left side of the wrapper to the center. Brush the top edge of the wrapper with some water and roll up tightly. Repeat with the remaining wrappers and filling.

6. Put the finished rolls, seam-side down, on the prepared baking sheet. Brush the rolls with the vegetable oil.

7. Bake for 20 to 25 minutes, turning the rolls halfway through the baking time, until browned and crispy.

8. Let the rolls cool before placing them in a zip-top bag to freeze.

IN THE MORNING

Microwave 2 spring rolls, covered, for 1 to 2 minutes. Put them in a bento box.

Variation tip: Spring roll wrappers are very versatile. You can use anything you want for the filling, such as chicken, beef, pork, fish, shellfish, asparagus, avocado, potato, rice noodle, egg, cheese, and so on—even chocolate or banana can be used to make a dessert wrap.

Per serving (2 spring rolls): Calories: 179; Total fat: 4g; Sodium: 618mg; Cholesterol: 19mg; Total carbs: 29g; Fiber: 1g; Sugar: 2g; Protein: 7g

GOMOKU-MAME (SIMMERED BEANS)

Gomoku-mame *is a traditional Japanese bean side dish that is based on Buddhist con-cepts. The main ingredients are simple, just vegetables and beans, but the dish is flavorful and nutritious. Japanese Buddhist cuisine was created to increase the energy of samu-rai, so the Japanese diet contains many well-balanced, energizing ingredients eaten in moderation.*

STORAGE: Up to 5 days in the refrigerator

PREP TIME: 5 min
COOK TIME: 35 min

3 shiitake mushrooms (or any mushrooms you like), stemmed and chopped

1 carrot, chopped

1½ cups water

6 tablespoons Versatile Sauce (page 136)

1 teaspoon Shimaya kombu dashi soup stock powder or any vegetable- or fish-based dashi powder

1 (15.5-ounce) can great northern beans, rinsed and drained

THE NIGHT BEFORE

1. In a saucepan, stir together the mushrooms, carrot, water, Versatile Sauce, and dashi powder. Bring to a boil over medium-low heat, reduce the heat medium-low, and simmer for 15 minutes. Stir and skim off the foam occasionally.

2. Add the beans and simmer for 5 minutes more. Turn off the heat and let sit for 10 minutes.

3. Transfer the beans and sauce to a clean container, and let cool before covering and refrigerating.

IN THE MORNING

Drain the excess liquid from the simmered beans and put one-fifth of them in the bento box.

Storage tip: Refrigerate the beans in the sauce so they soak up the liquid. This enhances their flavor.

Per serving: Calories: 99; Total fat: 0g; Sodium: 519mg; Cholesterol: 0mg; Total carbs: 20g; Fiber: 4g; Sugar: 5g; Protein: 5g

CUCUMBER SUSHI ROLLS BENTO

This bento may surprise you, because I put sushi rolls with two other recipes you may have never heard of. The cucumber sushi rolls, ginger chicken, and sweet tofu salad may sound like an impressive array, but as you will see, they are not difficult to make, and their flavors are out-of-this-world delicious. This bento has both sweet and savory tastes, so choose fruits or vegetables with lighter flavors as complementary extras.

TIMING & PREP

Cucumber Sushi Rolls (page 53): Make the night before (15 minutes) and keep covered with paper towels in the vegetable compartment of the refrigerator overnight.

Ginger Chicken (page 55): Make ahead (32 minutes) and refrigerate for up to 4 days.

Sweet Tofu Salad (page 56): Make ahead (15 minutes) and refrigerate for up to 3 days.

In the morning: Microwave the chicken, covered, for 30 seconds. Meanwhile, cut the sushi. Combine the chicken and sushi with the cold tofu salad in a bento box.

Easy extra suggestions: berries, grape tomatoes, hardboiled egg halves

CUCUMBER SUSHI ROLLS

Get ready for the easiest sushi roll recipe ever. There is no burdensome process and no need for special tools. All you need is cucumber, rice, nori seaweed sheets, and seasoning. You can make this the night before and cut the rolls in the morning. Vary the filling by using asparagus, carrot, avocado, and/or green beans. Cooked meat adds flavor.

STORAGE: 1 night (in the vegetable compartment of the refrigerator)

PREP TIME: 15 min

1 serving frozen Steamed Rice (page 134)

1½ teaspoons rice vinegar

¼ teaspoon sugar

Pinch salt

1 (7-by-8-inch) sheet nori seaweed, halved crosswise

1 baby cucumber, sliced

THE NIGHT BEFORE

1. Microwave the frozen rice for 2 to 3 minutes and put it in a small bowl. Stir in the vinegar, sugar, and salt.

2. Put a piece of parchment paper (slightly bigger than the nori) on a clean, dry work surface, and lay one piece of nori on it, horizontally. Using wet hands or a spoon, spread half the rice over the nori. Put half the cucumber slices on the rice. Pick up the edge of the parchment and roll it up like a jelly roll. Hold the roll tightly to form a good shape. Make another roll with the remaining ingredients.

3. Wrap each roll in a paper towel, and store them in the vegetable compartment of the refrigerator.

continued

CUCUMBER SUSHI ROLLS continued

IN THE MORNING

Cut the sushi rolls into 1-inch pieces and put them in a bento box.

Cooking tip: When you roll the nori, hold the edge of the parchment paper the whole time so you don't roll the paper into the sushi roll.

Tool tip: If you have a bamboo sushi mat, or *makisu,* use it instead of the parchment.

Substitution tip: Use thin pan-fried egg wrappers instead of the nori. Pour ½ a beaten egg into a greased, preheated 8-inch nonstick skillet. Spread the egg all over the surface of the pan to make a thin layer. Cook over medium-low heat for 3 minutes, gently flipping halfway through the cooking time. Making thin fried-egg wrappers is not complicated, and we use them a lot in many Japanese recipes, so it's a useful skill to master!

Per serving: Calories: 309; Total fat: 0g; Sodium: 164mg; Cholesterol: 0mg; Total carbs: 66g; Fiber: 4g; Sugar: 4g; Protein: 7g

GINGER CHICKEN

This is an incredibly flavorful chicken dish, marinated mainly with ginger and soy sauce. Traditional recipes use thinly sliced pork, but I prefer boneless, skinless chicken thighs because it they are juicier and more delicious. Ginger is extremely healthy, so I always keep some in the freezer. I peel fresh ginger with a spoon, wrap it in foil, and freeze it for up to 1 month. I can then grate the frozen ginger without thawing it first.

STORAGE: Up to 4 days in the refrigerator

PREP TIME: 20 min
COOK TIME: 12 min

4 boneless, skinless chicken thighs, cut into bite-size pieces

1 tablespoon grated peeled fresh ginger

¼ cup soy sauce (gluten free)

¼ cup cooking sake

2 tablespoons mirin

1 tablespoon toasted sesame oil

1 onion, sliced

THE NIGHT BEFORE

1. In a large bowl, combine the chicken, ginger, soy sauce, cooking sake, and mirin. Stir to coat the chicken with the sauce. Refrigerate to marinate for at least 15 minutes.

2. Meanwhile, in a skillet, heat the sesame oil over medium heat until it shimmers. Add the onion and sauté for 5 minutes.

3. Pour the chicken with the marinade into the skillet and cook, stirring, for about 7 minutes, until the chicken is cooked through.

4. Let cool before transferring to a clean container to refrigerate.

IN THE MORNING

Microwave one-fourth of the chicken, covered, for 30 seconds. Drain any excess sauce, and transfer the chicken to the bento box.

Per serving: Calories: 202; Total fat: 8g; Sodium: 1065mg; Cholesterol: 95mg; Total carbs: 8g; Fiber: 1g; Sugar: 3g; Protein: 23g

SWEET TOFU SALAD

You may have never heard of this traditional Japanese side dish. It is called shira-ae *in Japanese, and it comes from Buddhist cuisine. The ingredients are tofu and tender simmered vegetables, seasoned with sugar and soy sauce. I have loved this dish since I was a child, and I hope it becomes one of your new favorite salad recipes.*

STORAGE: Up to 3 days in the refrigerator

PREP TIME: 10 min
COOK TIME: 5 min

1 (14-ounce) package extra-firm tofu

3 shiitake mushrooms (or any mushrooms you like), stemmed and cut into small pieces

1 carrot, cut into small pieces

2 teaspoons plus 2 tablespoons soy sauce (gluten free if necessary), divided

1 teaspoon cooking sake

1 teaspoon Shimaya kombu dashi soup stock powder or any vegetable- or fish-based dashi powder

½ teaspoon salt, divided

2 cups water

2 tablespoons sugar

1 tablespoon roasted sesame seeds, ground

THE NIGHT BEFORE

1. Drain the tofu and wrap it in paper towels, then put it on a microwave-safe plate. Microwave for 3 minutes. Change the paper towels if they are completely soaked, then put a weight, such as a heavy plate, on the wrapped tofu for at least 10 minutes to drain completely.

2. Meanwhile, in a saucepan, stir together the mushrooms, carrot, 2 teaspoons of the soy sauce, cooking sake, dashi powder, ¼ teaspoon of salt, and water. Bring to a boil over medium heat, reduce the heat to maintain a simmer, and cook for 3 minutes.

3. Drain the vegetables and transfer to a clean kitchen towel to dry slightly.

4. In a large bowl, use your hands to roughly crumble the drained tofu. Stir in the sugar, sesame seeds, remaining soy sauce, remaining salt, and the drained vegetables. Transfer the salad to a clean container, then cover and refrigerate.

IN THE MORNING

Put one-third of the cold tofu salad in the bento box.

Tool tip: To grind sesame seeds, use a Japanese mortar and pestle or a clean spice grinder. If you don't have either, put the sesame seeds in a zip-top bag and crush them with a rolling pin.

Substitution tip: You can substitute firm tofu for the extra-firm kind. I use extra-firm tofu for food safety reasons. Extra-firm tofu contains less water than firm tofu, so it is less likely to drip or go bad.

Per serving: Calories: 194; Total fat: 9g; Sodium: 1209mg; Cholesterol: 0mg; Total carbs: 17g; Fiber: 2g; Sugar: 10g; Protein: 15g

TUNA SALAD SANDWICH BENTO PAGE 71

3

WESTERN-STYLE BENTOS

Do you like the idea of a bento lunch, but want to try it with non-Japanese dishes? This chapter teaches you how to do just that, using Western recipes in a bento format. Eating the comfort food you grew up with can have a calming and energizing impact—even on your busiest days. In this chapter, I will teach you how to prepare and pack familiar dishes in one bento box, while considering portion sizes and nutritional balance. Eating leftovers or the same food every day may be easy, but it can be boring and nutritionally unbalanced. The recipes in this chapter are prepared just for your lunch. Some can be made ahead, whereas others can be made in the morning in 10 minutes or less.

SPAGHETTI MARINARA BENTO

Yes! You can pack your favorite marinara sauce with spaghetti in a bento, along with egg muffins and sautéed asparagus and bacon. This bento is hearty and delicious. It is high in protein from the eggs and bacon and high in vitamins and minerals from the eggs, tomato sauce, and asparagus. Cooked spaghetti helps keep the bento safe because it absorbs excess moisture. In fact, Japanese store-bought bentos sometimes include boiled spaghetti at the bottom of the container as an edible desiccant. As this is a very colorful and nutritious bento, it is great by itself, or you can pack it along with your favorite small snack, like dried fruits and nuts.

TIMING & PREP

Spaghetti Marinara (page 61): Make ahead (12 minutes) and freeze for up to 3 weeks.

Breakfast Egg Muffins (page 62): Make ahead (35 minutes) and refrigerate for up to 3 days.

Sautéed Asparagus and Bacon (page 63): Cook in the morning (10 minutes).

In the morning: Cook the asparagus (10 minutes). Meanwhile, microwave the spaghetti, covered, for 2 to 3 minutes. Then, microwave the muffins for 30 seconds. Combine everything in a bento box.

Easy extra suggestions: dried fruits, nuts

SPAGHETTI MARINARA

Homemade frozen pasta dishes are very handy if you want to save time. The keys to freezing fresh spaghetti are to break the pasta in half before boiling it to prevent tangling, cook it to al dente, drain well, and dress with a sauce or oil before freezing. If you prefer, you can also coat your cooked pasta with oil, freeze it, and then mix it with the sauce in the morning when preparing the bento.

STORAGE: Up to
3 weeks in the freezer

PREP TIME: 2 min
COOK TIME: 10 min

Salt

8 ounces dried
spaghetti, broken in half

2 cups marinara sauce

Dried basil, for garnish

MAKE AHEAD

1. Fill a large saucepan with water and season with salt. Bring the water to a boil over high heat, add the spaghetti, and cook for 8 to 10 minutes, stirring occasionally, until al dente. Drain, transfer to a large bowl, and stir in the marinara.

2. Let cool. Divide the pasta into four portions, and transfer each portion to a zip-top bag or glass container to freeze.

IN THE MORNING

Microwave one serving for 2 to 3 minutes, covered, stirring halfway through the cooking time. Put the pasta in the bento box and sprinkle with basil.

Cooking tip: An easy way to measure the proper portion of dried spaghetti before cooking (about 2 ounces) is to use a regular water bottle cap. Fill the diameter of the cap with dried spaghetti. This is about one serving.

Per serving: Calories: 241; Total fat: 1g; Sodium: 645mg;
Cholesterol: 0mg; Total carbs: 49g; Fiber: 4g; Sugar: 7g; Protein: 9g

BREAKFAST EGG MUFFINS

Eggs are nutritious and easy to cook, but regular egg dishes can get boring. Of the many creative egg dishes out there, I think egg muffins are the best because they are easy to make ahead and not messy to eat. Many egg muffin recipes have tomatoes, spinach, and mushrooms, but these ingredients can make the muffins too moist for bentos. I use cheese and peas for my bento egg muffins because they are not too moist and are, of course, delicious.

STORAGE: Up to 3 days in the refrigerator

PREP TIME: 10 min
COOK TIME: 25 min

Nonstick cooking spray

6 large eggs

¼ cup frozen green peas

¼ cup shredded low-moisture mozzarella cheese

¼ teaspoon salt

¼ teaspoon freshly ground black pepper

THE NIGHT BEFORE

1. Preheat the oven to 350°F. Coat 6 cups of a standard muffin tin with cooking spray.

2. In a medium bowl, whisk together the eggs, peas, mozzarella cheese, salt, and pepper. Fill the muffin cups with the egg mixture, filling each about three-fourths full to prevent overflow.

3. Bake for 25 minutes or until the eggs are set and lightly browned on top.

4. Let cool. To remove the muffins, run a small knife along the inside edge of each muffin cup. Refrigerate in a zip-top bag.

IN THE MORNING

Microwave 2 muffins for 30 seconds and put them in the bento box.

Tool tip: Cooked egg sticks to the pan, so be sure to use a good-quality nonstick spray. I don't recommend using regular paper muffin cups because the paper sticks to the egg muffins and is hard to remove.

Per serving: Calories: 180; Total fat: 12g; Sodium: 401mg; Cholesterol: 377mg; Total carbs: 3g; Fiber: 1g; Sugar: 2g; Protein: 16g

SAUTÉED ASPARAGUS AND BACON

This is a very common, but nontraditional, bento dish in Japan. The only seasonings are salt and pepper, and you can cook this dish in the morning in about 10 minutes. I usually use turkey bacon, but you can use any kind of bacon or ham you like. If you don't have fresh asparagus, substitute frozen. There are no nutritional differences between fresh and frozen. In fact, frozen asparagus cooks more quickly.

PREP TIME: 3 min
COOK TIME: 7 min

1 tablespoon vegetable oil

3 asparagus stalks, trimmed and cut into 1-inch pieces

1 bacon slice, roughly chopped

Salt

Freshly ground black pepper

IN THE MORNING

In a skillet, heat the vegetable oil over medium heat until it shimmers. Add the asparagus and bacon and cook for 7 minutes or until they are both nicely soft. Season with salt and pepper, then transfer the asparagus and bacon to the bento box.

Storage tip: If you prefer to make this dish ahead, refrigerate it in an airtight container and use it within 3 days.

Per serving: Calories: 236; Total fat: 22g; Sodium: 595mg; Cholesterol: 21mg; Total carbs: 2g; Fiber: 1g; Sugar: 1g; Protein: 8g

RICE CROQUETTE BENTO

This "comfort food bento" is very filling. It contains rice croquettes, herb-seasoned roasted chicken, fresh celery and apple salad, and yummy chocolate fudge. Since chicken has high-quality protein and the croquette contains a good amount of carbs and protein from cheese, choose easy extras that are high in vitamins and low in carbs to make this bento even more nutritious.

TIMING & PREP

Rice Croquettes (page 65): Make ahead (50 minutes) and freeze for up to 3 weeks.

Oven-Roasted Chicken Thighs (page 67): Make ahead (50 minutes) and freeze for up to 3 weeks.

Celery and Apple Salad (page 68): Make ahead (10 minutes) and refrigerate for up to 2 days.

Chocolate Fudge (page 69): Make at least 4 days ahead (50 minutes) and refrigerate for up to 7 days.

In the morning: Microwave 3 croquettes, wrapped in a paper towel, for 90 seconds. Then, microwave 1 chicken thigh, wrapped in a paper towel, for 1 minute and slice it. Combine the croquettes and chicken with one serving each of the cold salad and fudge in a bento box.

Easy extra suggestions: cantaloupe, grape tomatoes, kiwi (halved; bring a spoon), mandarin oranges, radishes, raspberries, strawberries

RICE CROQUETTES

These mouthwatering croquettes have a crunchy outside and cheesy rice inside. The filling contains only cooked rice, cheese, and marinara sauce, so there is no need to take time to fry it all the way through using a lot of oil. When you reheat the frozen croquettes, use a microwave and then a toaster oven (if you have one). This keeps the texture crunchy, as if the croquettes were freshly fried. This dish is very party friendly; I recommend making a big batch ahead and freezing the extras so you can always be ready to reheat them and entertain on short notice.

STORAGE: Up to 3 weeks in the freezer

PREP TIME: 40 min
COOK TIME: 10 min

3 servings frozen Steamed Rice (page 134)

¾ cup marinara sauce

1 cup shredded mozzarella cheese

Salt

Freshly ground black pepper

2 tablespoons all-purpose flour

2 large eggs, beaten

½ cup bread crumbs

Vegetable oil, for frying

MAKE AHEAD

1. Microwave each portion of the frozen rice, covered, for 2 to 3 minutes. Transfer the rice to a large bowl and add the marinara sauce and mozzarella cheese. Stir to combine. Taste and season with salt and pepper as needed. Form the rice mixture into croquettes the size of golf balls.

2. Put the flour in a shallow bowl, the beaten eggs in a second shallow bowl, and the bread crumbs in a third bowl. One at a time, roll the croquettes in the flour, dip them into the egg, and press them into the bread crumbs. Tap off any excess breading.

3. In a deep pan, heat 2 inches of vegetable oil over medium heat until it shimmers. Add 4 croquettes at a time and fry, turning occasionally, until golden on all sides, about 2 minutes. Transfer to a wire rack to drain. Repeat with the remaining croquettes.

4. Let cool before transferring to a zip-top bag to freeze.

continued

RICE CROQUETTES continued

IN THE MORNING

Microwave 3 croquettes, wrapped in a paper towel, for 90 seconds, flipping halfway through the cooking time, and put them in a bento box. If you have a toaster oven, put the microwaved croquettes on a baking tray lined with foil. Toast them using the toast function until lightly browned.

Cooking tip: To check if the oil is hot enough to fry, drop some bread crumbs into the oil. If they float with bubbles, the oil is ready.

Safety tip: To fry the croquettes safely, use a deep pan for frying that has at least twice the height of the amount of oil used. While frying, put a metal strainer upside-down, like a lid, on the skillet. This prevents oil from spattering everywhere.

Per serving (3 croquettes): Calories: 152; Total fat: 8g; Sodium: 236mg; Cholesterol: 55mg; Total carbs: 9g; Fiber: 1g; Sugar: 2g; Protein: 4g

OVEN-ROASTED CHICKEN THIGHS

This is my husband's favorite recipe, and he cooks it in large quantities every other week. We keep them in the freezer all the time. The chicken is very juicy and has lots of flavor. In summer he likes to grill marinated chicken with barbecue sauce, but I prefer this recipe because I think it tastes better, and it avoids the unnecessary sugar sometimes found in barbecue sauces.

STORAGE: Up to 3 weeks in the freezer

PREP TIME: 15 min
COOK TIME: 35 min

Nonstick cooking spray

3 pounds boneless, skinless chicken thighs (about 8 thighs)

2 teaspoons Herb Seasoning (page 135)

MAKE AHEAD

1. Preheat the oven to 400°F. Coat a large baking dish with cooking spray.

2. Put the chicken thighs in the prepared baking dish and sprinkle with the seasoning.

3. Bake for 30 to 35 minutes, until cooked through. To check for doneness, make holes in the chicken using a toothpick or fork and check to be sure the juices run clear.

4. Let cool before transferring to a zip-top bag to freeze.

IN THE MORNING

Microwave 1 frozen chicken thigh, covered with paper towels, for 1 minute. Cut it into slices and transfer to the bento box.

Per serving: Calories: 195; Total fat: 7g; Sodium: 150mg; Cholesterol: 143mg; Total carbs: 0g; Fiber: 0g; Sugar: 0g; Protein: 33g

CELERY AND APPLE SALAD

This easy and refreshing salad pairs well with the other dishes in this bento. Celery is high in potassium and helps control the mineral balance of your body. It is a very versatile vegetable, but it does need a little care when storing: Separate the celery leaves from the ribs, and refrigerate the leaves in a zip-top bag. Wrap the stalks in a damp paper towel and refrigerate. Use the celery as soon as possible, definitely within about a week.

STORAGE: Up to 2 days in the refrigerator

PREP TIME: 10 min

1 Gala apple (or any apple you like), cored and chopped

3 celery stalks, chopped

6 fresh mint leaves, thinly sliced

Grated zest of 1 lemon, plus 2 teaspoons juice

1 tablespoon extra-virgin olive oil

Salt

Freshly ground black pepper

THE NIGHT BEFORE

In a medium bowl, stir together the apple, celery, mint, lemon zest and juice, and olive oil. Taste and season with salt and pepper as needed. Transfer to a clean container to refrigerate.

IN THE MORNING

Put half the cold salad in the bento box.

Per serving: Calories: 105; Total fat: 7g; Sodium: 99mg; Cholesterol: 0mg; Total carbs: 12g; Fiber: 3g; Sugar: 9g; Protein: 0g

EASY CHOCOLATE FUDGE

I created this easy recipe when my dear friend, Maiko, who lives in Italy, gave me a bar of Zaini Emilia extra-dark chocolate. Since then, I have experimented repeatedly with making easy, not-too-sweet chocolate fudge. The best recipe uses a 70 percent cacao chocolate bar (I recommend Lindt brand; it is easy to find). This recipe includes butter, sugar, and egg, so it has more calories than plain 70 percent chocolate, but even a small piece of fudge fills you up more and also makes you—or at least your taste buds—happy!

STORAGE: Up to 7 days in the refrigerator

PREP TIME: 10 min
COOK TIME: 40 min

Nonstick cooking spray

3½ ounces 70% cacao chocolate, finely chopped

4 tablespoons unsalted butter

1 tablespoon sugar

2 large eggs, beaten, at room temperature

MAKE AHEAD

1. Preheat the oven to 350°F. Coat a small (about 4-by-4-inch) baking pan with cooking spray.

2. In a small microwave-safe bowl, microwave the chocolate and butter for about 20 seconds, until the butter is melted. Whisk until the chocolate is also melted.

3. Stir in the sugar until well blended. Add a spoonful of the chocolate mixture to the beaten egg, and mix well to combine and temper the eggs. Whisk the eggs into the chocolate mixture. Pour the fudge into the prepared baking pan.

4. Bake for 25 minutes or until the top has formed a very thin crust, the edges are set, and the center is slightly bubbly and jiggly underneath if you give it a little shake.

5. Let the fudge sit for 15 minutes to set up, then refrigerate for at least 30 minutes before cutting and serving.

continued

IN THE MORNING

Cut the fudge into four pieces and put one piece in the bento box.

Cooking tip: If the chocolate isn't melted completely, heat it for 10 seconds more in the microwave.

Tool tip: It doesn't matter if the baking pan is square or round. All you need is a small size, about 4-by-4 inches, to make the fudge thick. If you can't find a small pan as described, make your own pan using doubled-over foil.

Per serving: Calories: 289; Total fat: 23g; Sodium: 117mg; Cholesterol: 124mg; Total carbs: 15g; Fiber: 3g; Sugar: 10g; Protein: 5g

TUNA SALAD SANDWICH BENTO

This bento boasts a perfect combination of taste, color, and nutrition. It includes a tuna salad sandwich, buttered corn, and pleasantly sour marinated vegetables. I recommend this bento when you want a light lunch. You can prepare the two vegetable dishes ahead and quickly make the sandwich in the morning. Add green fruits or veggies for easy extras; for more protein, add egg or cheese.

TIMING & PREP

Simple Tuna Salad Sandwich (page 72): Prepare in the morning (6 minutes).

Buttered Corn (page 73): Make ahead (12 minutes) and refrigerate for up to 3 days.

Marinated Radishes and Bell Peppers (page 75): Make ahead (5 minutes) and refrigerate for up to 4 days.

In the morning: Microwave the corn for 30 seconds. Prepare the sandwich (6 minutes). Combine the corn and sandwich with the cold marinated vegetables in a bento box.

Easy extra suggestions: cantaloupe, grape tomatoes, green grapes, hardboiled egg (halved), kiwi (halved; bring a spoon), stick cheese

SIMPLE TUNA SALAD SANDWICH

Mixing tuna and mayonnaise is one of the simplest ways to make a hearty dish. Sometimes tuna sandwiches include chopped onion, lettuce leaves, tomato, and so on. But this sandwich contains just tuna, mayo, and buttered bread. Fewer ingredients produce a softer, creamier (and more kid-friendly) sandwich. To keep the tuna mixture less watery (and therefore prevent the bread from getting soggy), make the sandwich in the morning from scratch—it takes only about 6 minutes. You can also mix in any seasonings you like, such as cayenne pepper, onion powder, dried basil, or dried oregano.

PREP TIME: 6 min

1 (5-ounce) can tuna packed in water, drained

2 tablespoons mayonnaise

Salt

Freshly ground black pepper

2 slices whole-grain bread or any bread you like

1½ teaspoons butter or margarine, at room temperature

IN THE MORNING

1. Wrap the drained tuna in paper towels and lightly blot to remove excess water. Transfer the tuna to a small bowl and stir in the mayo, mixing well. Taste and season with salt and pepper as needed.

2. Spread butter on one side of each piece of bread. Put the tuna mixture on the buttered side of one piece of bread. Cover the tuna with the other piece of bread, buttered-side down. Cut the sandwich in half and put it into the bento box.

Cooking tip: Spreading butter on the inside of the sandwich prevents the bread from soaking up excess moisture from the tuna mixture and becoming soggy.

Substitution tip: Use more mayo and/or mustard instead of butter to coat the bread.

Per serving: Calories: 489; Total fat: 29g; Sodium: 840mg; Cholesterol: 75mg; Total carbs: 23g; Fiber: 4g; Sugar: 3g; Protein: 33g

BUTTERED CORN

This quick recipe adds buttery flavor to other dishes such as rice, salad, or pasta. Here, I introduce you to the make-ahead version, but if you prefer, you can cook this in the morning—it requires just two ingredients. I use frozen sweet corn, which I always have on hand, and cook it over medium-high heat to cook off all the moisture. If you use fresh corn, cook it over medium-low heat.

STORAGE: Up to
3 days in the refrigerator

PREP TIME: 2 min
COOK TIME: 10 min

2 tablespoons butter or
margarine

3 cups frozen sweet
corn kernels

THE NIGHT BEFORE

In a skillet, melt the butter over medium-high heat. Add the corn and stir-fry for 8 to 10 minutes to evaporate the water from the frozen corn. Transfer to a clean container to refrigerate.

IN THE MORNING

Microwave half the corn for 30 seconds and add it to the bento box.

Ingredient tip: If you use unsalted butter, season the corn with salt during cooking.

Variation tip: Season with your favorite spices or herbs. If you like spicy flavors, try some red pepper flakes.

Per serving: Calories: 300; Total fat: 14g; Sodium: 116mg; Cholesterol: 31mg; Total carbs: 44g; Fiber: 6g; Sugar: 8g; Protein: 8g

MARINATED RADISHES AND BELL PEPPERS

This easy pickle-like recipe takes only 5 minutes to prepare. There is no need to cook the vegetables, as they become tender while marinating. The slightly sour vegetables go really well with sandwiches. It is better to marinate this dish for at least one night so the vegetables soak up the delicious dressing and the bitter taste of the radishes is tempered. I use radishes and bell peppers because they are high in vitamin C and potassium and add beautiful colors to the bento. Substitute shredded carrot, grape tomato, shredded cabbage, or celery, if you prefer.

STORAGE: Up to
4 days in the refrigerator

PREP TIME: 5 min

5 radishes, quartered

1 yellow bell pepper, cored and sliced

1 tablespoon extra-virgin olive oil

1 tablespoon white wine vinegar

½ teaspoon salt

¼ teaspoon freshly ground black pepper

¼ teaspoon sugar

THE NIGHT BEFORE

In a food storage container, stir together the radishes, yellow bell pepper, olive oil, vinegar, salt, pepper, and sugar until well mixed. Refrigerate at least overnight to marinate.

IN THE MORNING

Put one-third of the cold marinated vegetables in the bento box.

Ingredient tip: It is okay if the olive oil becomes light yellow and has solidified into small lumps during refrigeration. They will melt by lunchtime.

Per serving: Calories: 61; Total fat: 5g; Sodium: 392mg; Cholesterol: 0mg; Total carbs: 5g; Fiber: 1g; Sugar: 1g; Protein: 1g

MINI MEATBALL BENTO

Both young and old will love this quick and easy bento. It contains a creamy egg sandwich, comforting mini chicken meatballs, and carrot salad with Parmesan cheese. Cook the meatballs and salad ahead of time, and make the sandwich in the morning. This bento is very high in protein and vitamins. Add a pop of green with your easy extras.

TIMING & PREP

Quick Creamy Egg Sandwich (page 77): Prepare in the morning (6 minutes).

Mini Chicken Meatballs (page 78): Make ahead (45 minutes) and freeze for up to 3 weeks.

Carrot Salad with Parmesan Cheese (page 80): Make ahead (10 minutes) and refrigerate for up to 4 days.

In the morning: Microwave 3 or 4 meatballs, covered, for 90 seconds. Meanwhile, prepare the sandwich (5 minutes). Combine the meatballs and the sandwich with the cold carrot salad in a bento box.

Easy extra suggestions: cantaloupe, green grapes, kiwi (halved; bring a spoon)

QUICK CREAMY EGG SANDWICH

This is a fuss-free recipe if you have hardboiled eggs and mayonnaise in your refrigerator. I love this recipe because it doesn't include unnecessary ingredients, and the sandwich is so soft and creamy. I like to keep things super simple so the ingredients shine! If you don't have store-bought or precooked hardboiled eggs, cook 1 large egg in boiling water over medium heat for 12 minutes, then peel it under cold running water.

PREP TIME: 6 min

1 large hardboiled egg, peeled

1 tablespoon mayonnaise

Pinch salt

Pinch freshly ground black pepper

1½ teaspoons butter or margarine, at room temperature

2 slices whole-grain bread or any bread you like

IN THE MORNING

1. In a small bowl, use a fork to mash together the egg and mayo, crumbling the egg and mixing it with the mayo. Season with salt and pepper and mix to combine.

2. Spread butter on one side of each piece of bread. Put the egg mixture on the buttered side of a piece of bread. Cover the egg mixture with the other piece of bread, buttered-side down. Cut the sandwich in half and put it in a bento box.

Per serving: Calories: 350; Total fat: 23g; Sodium: 620mg; Cholesterol: 206mg; Total carbs: 24g; Fiber: 4g; Sugar: 4g; Protein: 14g

MINI CHICKEN MEATBALLS

This is such a bento-friendly dish! The easy pan-fried meatballs are smaller than golf balls and both delicious and hearty. It is also a pretty presentation if you thread the meatballs onto colorful skewers. Cooking homemade meatballs is your opportunity to get any picky eaters in your family to eat their vegetables—finely mince the onion (or other vegetables) and mix it into the chicken mixture. Nobody will know the difference, but everyone will get the nutrition! For bento safety, there is no watery sauce covering the meatballs—which also allows you to be more generous with the seasoning, if you choose.

STORAGE: Up to
3 weeks in the freezer

PREP TIME: 15 min
COOK TIME: 30 min

1 pound
ground chicken

1 small onion,
finely chopped

1 large egg, beaten

½ cup bread crumbs

Salt

Freshly ground
black pepper

1 tablespoon
vegetable oil

MAKE AHEAD

1. In a medium bowl, combine the ground chicken, onion, egg, and bread crumbs, and season with salt and pepper. Mix for at least 2 minutes, until very well combined. Shape the chicken mixture into balls slightly smaller than golf balls.

2. In a skillet, heat the vegetable oil over medium heat until it shimmers. Add 6 or 7 meatballs at a time, and cook for 3 minutes. Flip the meatballs, reduce the heat to low, and cover the skillet. Cook for 7 minutes more. Repeat with the remaining meatballs.

3. Let cool before transferring to a zip-top bag to freeze.

IN THE MORNING

Microwave 3 or 4 meatballs, covered, for 90 seconds; skewer 2 each on 2 skewers if you'd like; and then pack them in the bento box.

Tool tip: If the meat mixture is too soft to shape with your hands, use two spoons to make balls and drop them into the skillet. Or use a small ice cream scoop or melon baller, if you have one.

Safety tip: To make sure the meat is cooked through, make a few holes on the surface using a toothpick and check to be sure the juices run clear. If it is undercooked, cook for a few more minutes over low heat with the lid on until the juices run clear.

Per serving (4 meatballs): Calories: 195; Total fat: 11g; Sodium: 140mg; Cholesterol: 114mg; Total carbs: 6g; Fiber: 1g; Sugar: 1g; Protein: 18g

CARROT SALAD WITH PARMESAN CHEESE

In this dish, shredded carrot is lightly sautéed and seasoned with salt and pepper. Parmesan cheese adds a finishing touch. It is much more satisfying than eating raw carrot. I prefer to cook the carrot in a pan on the stovetop because our bodies can absorb more beta carotene from the carrot when we cook it with oil, but if you'd like, you can cook it in the microwave, covered, for about 1 minute.

STORAGE: Up to 4 days in the refrigerator

PREP TIME: 5 min
COOK TIME: 5 min

1 tablespoon olive oil

2 large carrots, shredded

Salt

Freshly ground black pepper

2 tablespoons grated Parmesan cheese

½ teaspoon dried basil

MAKE AHEAD

1. In a skillet, heat the olive oil over medium heat until it shimmers. Add the carrot and cook, stirring, for 3 minutes. Season with salt and pepper to taste.

2. Transfer to a clean container and stir in the cheese and basil. Let cool, then cover and refrigerate.

IN THE MORNING

Put one-fourth of the cold salad in the bento box.

Cooking tip: If you don't have a grater for shredding the carrots, cut them into very thin slices so they become tender while sautéing.

Per serving: Calories: 56; Total fat: 4g; Sodium: 96mg; Cholesterol: 3mg; Total carbs: 4g; Fiber: 1g; Sugar: 2g; Protein: 1g

CHICKEN ROLL BENTO

I know many people bring ham and cheese sandwiches for lunch, but in this recipe, I introduce you to a nutritious and delicious pairing to step up your ham sandwich game with chicken rolls and an easy salad. This bento contains lots of protein, vitamins, minerals, and good fat.

TIMING & PREP

Turkey Ham and Cheese Sandwich (page 82): Make ahead (12 minutes) and freeze, wrapped in plastic wrap, for up to 3 weeks.

Microwaved Chicken Rolls (page 83): Make ahead (35 minutes), cut, and freeze for up to 3 weeks.

Spinach and Walnut Salad (page 85): Make ahead (6 minutes) and refrigerate for up to 4 days.

In the morning: Microwave 3 chicken rolls, covered, for 50 seconds. Put them in a bento box with the frozen sandwich (it will thaw by lunchtime) and cold salad.

Easy extra suggestions: apple, banana, cherries, grapes

TURKEY HAM AND CHEESE SANDWICH

For bento safety and for saving time in the morning, this sandwich is made ahead and frozen. I know that may seem odd, but the sandwich will thaw by lunchtime. The keys to success here are using no watery ingredients in the sandwich and wrapping it in plastic wrap. I try not to use plastic wrap when possible, so I have been experimenting with other wrappers to keep the right texture after thawing—but so far, plastic wrap is the winner.

STORAGE: Up to 3 weeks in the freezer

PREP TIME: 10 min
COOK TIME: 2 min

4 thin slices turkey ham or any ham you like

6 teaspoons butter or margarine, at room temperature

8 slices whole-grain bread or any bread you like

4 slices provolone, or any cheese you like

MAKE AHEAD

1. In a dry skillet, cook the ham over medium heat for 2 minutes, flipping it halfway through the cooking time. Let cool completely.

2. Spread butter on one side of each piece of bread. Lay 1 slice of cheese and 1 slice of ham on the buttered side of 4 slices. Cover the ham and cheese with the other pieces of bread, buttered-side down.

3. Cut the sandwiches in half, wrap each half very tightly in plastic wrap, and freeze.

IN THE MORNING

Put 2 wrapped sandwich halves, still frozen, in a bento box.

Cooking tip: Let the ham cool completely after cooking. Use the refrigerator to help it cool if you are pressed for time. The heat from cooked ham makes the bread soggy when it thaws.

Storage tip: Wrap the sandwiches tightly, with no air between the bread and the plastic, so no frost develops.

Per serving: Calories: 308; Total fat: 15g; Sodium: 895mg; Cholesterol: 43mg; Total carbs: 25g; Fiber: 4g; Sugar: 3g; Protein: 19g

MICROWAVED CHICKEN ROLLS

This easy, delicious chicken tenderloin dish with green beans and carrot requires no messy cleanup. You don't need to heat oil in a pan or even preheat your oven—just prepare the ingredients and microwave them. You can use chicken thighs or breasts instead, but they will need more time to cook in the microwave (and thaw in the morning) than the tenderloin.

STORAGE: Up to 3 weeks in the freezer

PREP TIME: 15 min
COOK TIME: 20 min

5 pieces chicken tenderloin

Salt

Freshly ground black pepper

10 green beans, trimmed

½ carrot, cut into 2-inch-long thin strips

MAKE AHEAD

1. Butterfly the chicken tenderloins by making an incision from the side, without cutting all the way through. Open the pieces like a book and pound with a rolling pin or meat tenderizer until they're ⅛ to ¼ inch thick, or as thin as possible. Generously season with salt and pepper.

2. Put the chicken horizontally on a work surface. Arrange about 2 pieces each of green bean and carrot straight down the middle of the chicken, then roll it up. Repeat with the remaining chicken and vegetables.

3. Place one roll in the middle of an 8-inch square piece of parchment paper and roll it up. Fold the excess side paper to the seam side. Repeat with the remaining chicken rolls.

continued

4. Place the wrapped rolls, seam-side down, on a microwave-safe plate and microwave for 5 minutes. Let sit for 15 minutes at room temperature.

5. Cut each roll into 3 pieces and transfer them to a zip-top bag to freeze.

IN THE MORNING

Microwave 3 chicken rolls, covered, for 50 seconds and put them in a bento box.

Cooking tip: When you cut the cooked chicken rolls, check inside to make sure the chicken is cooked through. If not, microwave the cut chicken for 10 seconds more and let cool.

Per serving: Calories: 73; Total fat: 1g; Sodium: 64mg; Cholesterol: 20mg; Total carbs: 8g; Fiber: 4g; Sugar: 2g; Protein: 10g

SPINACH AND WALNUT SALAD

This is not a typical baby spinach salad. The baby spinach is cooked, but only for 10 seconds, which gives it a tender texture. Baby spinach contains less oxalic acid than regular spinach, so we can enjoy it raw or quickly blanched. If you use regular spinach, boil it for 2 minutes to get the same taste and texture as baby spinach.

STORAGE: Up to 4 days in the refrigerator

PREP TIME: 5 min
COOK TIME: 1 min

10 ounces fresh baby spinach

¼ cup walnut pieces

Grated zest of 1 lemon

1 teaspoon extra-virgin olive oil

Salt

Freshly ground black pepper

MAKE AHEAD

1. Bring a small pot of water to a boil over high heat. Blanch the spinach for 10 seconds in the boiling water, then drain. Lay the spinach on paper towels, and use more paper towels to blot it until almost dry. Transfer to a medium bowl.

2. Add the walnuts, lemon zest, and olive oil, and season with salt and pepper. Toss to combine, and transfer the salad to a clean container to refrigerate.

IN THE MORNING

Put one-third of the cold salad in the bento box.

Per serving: Calories: 95; Total fat: 8g; Sodium: 125mg; Cholesterol: 0mg; Total carbs: 4g; Fiber: 3g; Sugar: 1g; Protein: 4g

BAKED ZITI BENTO

I have loved baked ziti since I first came to the United States, and I have taught many Japanese friends how to cook this bento because it is very hearty, filling, and tasty. Remember, some foods lose subtle flavor when they are frozen because their cell walls break down and the ingredients lose moisture. That's why I recommend seasoning slightly more liberally when cooking bento recipes that will be frozen. This bento has no meat, so it is great for vegetarians. For your easy extras, add red fruits or veggies that are low in carbs and high in vitamins and minerals.

TIMING & PREP

Easy Baked Ziti Casserole (page 87): Make ahead (40 minutes) and freeze for up to 3 weeks.

Roasted Potatoes, Carrots, and Broccoli (page 89): Make ahead (50 minutes) and freeze for up to 3 weeks.

Fluffy Scrambled Eggs with Green Peas (page 91): Cook in the morning (5 minutes).

In the morning: Microwave the ziti, covered, for 2 to 3 minutes. Then, cook the egg (5 minutes) and microwave the roasted vegetables for 3 minutes. Combine all the dishes in a bento box.

Easy extra suggestions: berries, grape tomatoes, radishes

EASY BAKED ZITI CASSEROLE

This is the first dish my husband ever cooked for me. The recipe doesn't contain egg or meat—just ziti, lots of cheese, and marinara sauce. The keys to reheating frozen baked ziti while maintaining a freshly cooked taste are to divide the ziti into small portions before freezing and to stir occasionally while microwaving. In the microwave, food on the edge of the plate cooks first, and food in the center of the plate is the last to cook. Once you know this rule, your reheat time may get shorter and your results will be better.

STORAGE: Up to 3 weeks in the freezer

PREP TIME: 10 min
COOK TIME: 30 min

Nonstick cooking spray

Salt

1 pound dried ziti

1 (24-ounce) jar marinara sauce

1 (15-ounce) tub ricotta cheese

2 cups shredded mozzarella cheese, divided

MAKE AHEAD

1. Preheat the oven to 375°F. Coat a large casserole dish with cooking spray.

2. Meanwhile, bring a large pot of water to a boil over high heat, and season it with salt. Add the ziti and cook for slightly less time than the package directions for al dente (so the ziti is not quite al dente).

3. In a large bowl, stir together the marinara sauce, ricotta, and 1½ cups of mozzarella cheese.

4. Drain the pasta, add it to the bowl, and stir to combine. Transfer the pasta mixture to the prepared casserole dish.

5. Bake for 20 minutes. Top with the remaining ½ cup of mozzarella cheese and bake for 5 minutes more or until the cheese melts. Let cool.

continued

6. Cut the pasta into 16 equal-size squares and put 2 squares in each zip-top bag to freeze.

IN THE MORNING

Put 2 frozen squares toward the opposite outer edges of a microwave-safe plate. Microwave, covered, for 2 to 3 minutes, stirring halfway through the cooking time. Place the squares in your bento box.

Cooking tip: Warm the ziti before eating, if possible, for better flavor.

Per serving: Calories: 374; Total fat: 11g; Sodium: 711mg; Cholesterol: 31mg; Total carbs: 51g; Fiber: 4g; Sugar: 6g; Protein: 21g

ROASTED POTATOES, CARROTS, AND BROCCOLI

Roasting is a great way to prepare vegetables. It is fuss free and delivers delicious results. Here, I teach you to make roasted vegetables that can be frozen for easy use. I use potato, carrot, and broccoli. Because broccoli takes a shorter time to cook than potato and carrot, the recipe requires that you add the broccoli halfway through the roasting time. You can use other vegetables, but keep in mind that veggies such as zucchini, pepper, or tomato can get mushy after reheating—I generally avoid those for this recipe.

STORAGE: Up to 3 weeks in the freezer

PREP TIME: 10 min
COOK TIME: 40 min

10 Yukon Gold potatoes, scrubbed and cut into 1-inch cubes

2 carrots, cut into ½-inch-thick pieces

4 teaspoons Herb Seasoning (page 135)

1 tablespoon vegetable oil

2 broccoli crowns, cut into small florets

MAKE AHEAD

1. Preheat the oven to 400°F.

2. In a large bowl, combine the potatoes, carrots, seasoning, and vegetable oil. Toss to coat. Spread the potatoes and carrots in an even layer on a large rimmed baking sheet.

3. Roast for 20 minutes.

4. Add the broccoli, tossing and stirring to coat it in the oil and spices. Roast for 20 minutes more.

5. Let cool. Divide the vegetables into 6 equal portions, and put each portion in a zip-top bag to freeze.

continued

IN THE MORNING

Put the frozen carrots and broccoli in the middle of a microwave-safe plate, and put the frozen potatoes on the outer edges of the plate. (The potato takes more time to reheat, and the other vegetables will dry out when reheating the potato unless separated.) Microwave for 3 minutes, stirring halfway through the cooking time, and transfer to your bento box.

Per serving: Calories: 304; Total fat: 3g; Sodium: 65mg; Cholesterol: 0mg; Total carbs: 64g; Fiber: 11g; Sugar: 7g; Protein: 9g

FLUFFY SCRAMBLED EGGS WITH GREEN PEAS

Do you stir all the time when you cook scrambled eggs? If you like a soft, fluffy texture, you need a little patience. You cook this dish in the morning, so you may be tempted to rush the eggs along, but stirring doesn't save you any time and actually hurts the texture of the eggs. I recommend mild seasoning for this dish because both the ziti and the roasted vegetables have a lot of flavor. Enjoy the natural taste of the eggs and green peas.

PREP TIME: 2 min
COOK TIME: 3 min

1 tablespoon butter or margarine

¼ cup frozen green peas

2 large eggs

Pinch salt

Pinch freshly ground black pepper

IN THE MORNING

1. In a skillet, melt the butter over medium heat. Add the peas and cook for 1 minute.

2. Meanwhile, in a small bowl, whisk together the eggs, salt, and pepper. Pour the eggs into the skillet. Cook without stirring until the edges of the eggs are slightly cooked. Reduce the heat to low. Using a spatula, gently gather the cooked part toward the center of the skillet and spread the uncooked egg toward the edge of the pan. Fold the edges over onto themselves until cooked all the way through. Transfer the eggs and peas to the bento box.

Per serving: Calories: 274; Total fat: 21g; Sodium: 430mg; Cholesterol: 372mg; Total carbs: 6g; Fiber: 2g; Sugar: 3g; Protein: 15g

QUINOA BOWL BENTO

This bento includes quinoa salad and an eggless tofu muffin. It is nice for people who follow a vegan diet, but even the most dedicated meat eaters will love it, too. Because both dishes contain tofu, this bento is high in protein, and it's also high in vitamins from the vegetables. Pack the almond dressing for the quinoa salad in a separate container to keep all the ingredients in the bento crunchy. Since the muffin contains sugar, add fruits that have comparatively less sugar for your easy extras.

TIMING & PREP

Quinoa Salad (page 93): Make the quinoa and vegetables the night before, and assemble them in a bento box (30 minutes). Then, make the dressing and put it in a small separate container (5 minutes). Cover and refrigerate.

Eggless Tofu Muffins (page 94): Make ahead (40 minutes) and freeze for up to 3 weeks.

In the morning: Pack the salad, dressing, and frozen muffins (they will thaw by lunchtime) in the bento box.

Easy extra suggestions: berries, kiwi (halved; bring a spoon), mandarin oranges

QUINOA SALAD

No more boring salads! This dish is so versatile—add whatever flavors you like, using different vegetables as the topping. The almond butter dressing is quick to make and very flavorful (use a little warm water to adjust the consistency).

STORAGE: Overnight in the refrigerator

PREP TIME: 15 min
COOK TIME: 20 min

¼ cup quinoa, rinsed well

1 tablespoon no-sugar-added and no-salt-added almond butter

Juice of ½ lemon

¼ teaspoon salt

Freshly ground black pepper

Onion powder

2 to 3 tablespoons warm water, as needed

¼ (14-ounce) package firm tofu, cubed

½ cup small broccoli florets

¼ cup frozen sweet corn kernels

½ red bell pepper, chopped

½ cup baby arugula, chopped

THE NIGHT BEFORE

1. Cook the quinoa according to the package directions and set aside to cool.

2. In a small bowl, whisk together the almond butter, lemon juice, and salt; season with pepper and onion powder to taste. Whisk in the warm water until you have a consistency you like. Transfer to a small container and refrigerate.

3. In a dry skillet, cook the tofu and broccoli over medium heat for about 5 minutes, until they are slightly browned.

4. Transfer the cooked and cooled quinoa to the bento box and top with the tofu, broccoli, frozen corn, bell pepper, and arugula. Refrigerate.

IN THE MORNING

Add the dressing to the bento box.

Variation tip: If you are not following a vegan diet, add cooked egg, fish, or chicken to this salad. Also, add any spices you like to make your favorite dressing—soy sauce, sesame oil, rice vinegar, and/or curry powder provide a lot of Asian flavor.

Per serving: Calories: 342; Total fat: 13g; Sodium: 621mg; Cholesterol: 0mg; Total carbs: 47g; Fiber: 9g; Sugar: 7g; Protein: 15g

EGGLESS TOFU MUFFINS

In Japan, it is common to add tofu to various dishes, such as meatballs, pancakes, and so on. It makes the dishes fluffier and healthier, and using tofu requires fewer other ingredients. I experimented with making tofu muffins many times to get just the right texture and taste. I have come up with a delicious muffin that you would never know contained tofu. You can make these ahead and pop them into the freezer. In the morning, just bring them along with you—they will thaw by lunchtime.

STORAGE: Up to 3 weeks in the freezer

PREP TIME: 15 min
COOK TIME: 25 min

4 tablespoons unsalted butter, at room temperature

2 tablespoons vegetable oil

¼ (14-ounce) package firm tofu, crumbled

1 cup sugar

1½ cups all-purpose flour

1 teaspoon baking powder

½ cup plus 2 tablespoons almond milk

1 teaspoon vanilla extract

MAKE AHEAD

1. Preheat the oven to 375°F. Line a standard muffin tin with paper liners.

2. In a medium bowl, using a handheld electric mixer, beat together the butter, vegetable oil, tofu, and sugar until creamy.

3. Add the flour and baking powder. Mix together while gradually pouring in the almond milk. Mix in the vanilla until combined. Using a large spoon, scoop the batter into the prepared cups, filling each cup a little more than three-fourths full.

4. Bake for 25 minutes or until a toothpick inserted into the center of a muffin comes out clean.

5. Let the muffins cool before transferring them to a large zip-top bag to freeze.

IN THE MORNING

Pack 1 or 2 muffins, still frozen, in a bento box.

Cooking tip: If you are sensitive to tofu's aroma, add freshly squeezed lemon juice to the crumbled tofu to remove the tofu smell completely.

Substitution tip: Use any kind of milk, sugar, and oil you like. I prefer coconut oil, which makes the muffins even tastier.

Per serving (1 muffin): Calories: 180; Total fat: 7g; Sodium: 43mg; Cholesterol: 10mg; Total carbs: 29g; Fiber: 1g; Sugar: 17g; Protein: 2g

PERFECT TRICOLORED BENTO PAGE 98

FUSION BENTOS

Japan has a rich food culture, but over the years, Japanese people have created new recipes inspired, in part, by foreign food cultures. These fusion dishes are delicious! Japanese chefs add Japanese elements to foreign dishes or foreign elements to Japanese dishes, adjusting the flavors, serving size, and final presentation to meet Japanese standards. Ingredients are often changed to be fresher because Japanese people believe natural food is healthier.

In this chapter I introduce you to nontraditional, but popular, Japanese fusion bentos. Some dishes in this chapter may be familiar, and others may not be. Either way, you will definitely love these fusion treasures.

PERFECT TRICOLORED BENTO

Traditional Japanese meals feature different colors combined in an easy way to create well-balanced plates. In Japan, there is a popular three-colored rice bowl recipe that consists of sautéed chicken crumbles, scrambled egg, and boiled spinach. The ingredients in that meal are very different from this bento, but this bento accentuates the Japanese tradition of putting many colors into a meal, with green from asparagus and peas, red from salmon, ham, and ketchup, and yellow from egg. Add green or yellow fruits or veggies to create an even more colorful presentation.

TIMING & PREP

Loaded Rice with Ham and Peas (page 99): Make ahead (85 minutes) and freeze for up to 3 weeks.

Simple Egg Salad (page 101): Make ahead (10 minutes) and refrigerate for up to 3 days.

Sautéed Asparagus and Salmon (page 103): Make ahead (20 minutes) and refrigerate for up to 5 days.

In the morning: Microwave the rice, covered, for 2 to 3 minutes. Then, microwave the salmon, covered, for 30 seconds. Combine the rice and salmon with half the cold egg salad in a bento box.

Easy extra suggestions: cantaloupe, green grapes, kiwi (halved; bring a spoon), mandarin oranges

LOADED RICE WITH HAM AND PEAS

I know this is a very strange dish for people who are not used to Japanese-style Western food. Japanese cooks often use ketchup like tomato sauce for Western dishes. But trust me, this dish is very popular in Japan. Slightly browning the ketchup adds lots of flavor. Japanese bentos often contain ham or bacon, usually in very small amounts, but you can use any kind of meat you choose for this dish. Just be sure to cook any meat well, because bento meat must be cooked all the way through for safety.

STORAGE: Up to 3 weeks in the freezer

PREP TIME: 40 min
COOK TIME: 45 min

1½ cups uncooked short-grain white rice

1⅔ cups water

1 tablespoon vegetable oil

2 ounces turkey ham, cut into small pieces

½ cup frozen green peas

1 cup ketchup

Pinch salt

Pinch freshly ground black pepper

MAKE AHEAD

1. In a fine-mesh strainer set atop a bowl, rinse the rice under cool running water while stirring it with your hand. Drain the rice as soon as the water in the bowl turns a murky white color. Repeat until the water in the bowl is clear.

2. In a medium bowl, combine the rice and water; let soak for 30 minutes at room temperature.

3. Pour the rice with the soaking water into a deep saucepan. Cover and bring to a boil over high heat, about 5 minutes. Turn the heat to very low and cook for 10 to 12 minutes. When there is no water left in the pan, turn the heat off, put a kitchen towel under the lid, and steam for 10 minutes. This makes the rice softer.

continued

4. In a large skillet or wok, heat the vegetable oil over medium heat until it shimmers. Add the ham and peas and cook for 1 minute.

5. Add the ketchup and cook, stirring, for 2 minutes.

6. Add the cooked rice, season with salt and pepper, and stir-fry for 4 minutes or until the rice is coated with the ketchup.

7. Let cool. Divide the rice mixture into four portions, and transfer each portion to a zip-top bag or glass container to freeze.

IN THE MORNING

Microwave one portion of the frozen rice, covered, for 2 to 3 minutes, then transfer it to a bento box.

Cooking tip: Before putting a kitchen towel over the rice, check inside the pan. If there is still water in the pan, put the lid back on and cook for 2 more minutes, then check again.

Ingredient tip: If you have stored Steamed Rice (page 134) in your freezer, microwave one portion of the frozen rice in the morning, then stir-fry it with one-fourth of the other ingredients.

Per serving: Calories: 389; Total fat: 5g; Sodium: 838mg; Cholesterol: 9mg; Total carbs: 78g; Fiber: 3g; Sugar: 15g; Protein: 9g

SIMPLE EGG SALAD

In Japan, egg salad is made a variety of ways, usually with different chopped vegetables, such as onion, cabbage, or broccoli, and sometimes with macaroni or a protein such as shrimp, avocado, bacon, or cheese to make it more filling. This super-simple version is best for bento safety, as other ingredients, especially chopped vegetables, can add too much moisture. The salad is delicious on its own, but it's also good as a filling for croquettes. In Japan, we mix this salad with chopped pickles and use it like a sauce on fried fish and fried chicken.

STORAGE: Up to 3 days in refrigerator

PREP TIME: 5 min
COOK TIME: 5 min

3 large hardboiled eggs, peeled

2 tablespoons mayonnaise

Salt

Freshly ground black pepper

THE NIGHT BEFORE

In a medium bowl, using a fork, mash together the eggs and mayonnaise, crumbling the egg and mixing it with the mayo. Season with salt and pepper and mix to combine. Transfer to a clean container to refrigerate.

IN THE MORNING

Transfer half the cold egg salad to the bento box.

Ingredient tip: I recommend Japanese mayonnaise, Kewpie, which you can buy at many Asian markets or on Amazon. It tastes so good!

Substitution tip: If you don't have hardboiled eggs on hand, cook 3 eggs in boiling water over medium heat for 12 minutes, then peel them under cold running water.

Per serving: Calories: 197; Total fat: 18g; Sodium: 273mg; Cholesterol: 284mg; Total carbs: 1g; Fiber: 0g; Sugar: 1g; Protein: 9g

SAUTÉED ASPARAGUS AND SALMON

This quick and easy recipe produces an incredibly delicious dish. If you are tired of baked or grilled salmon, try this. It is flavorful and has a very soft texture because it is steamed with cooking sake. I recommend buying fresh salmon and freezing each fillet in a zip-top bag. Transfer the salmon to the refrigerator to thaw one day before you cook it.

STORAGE: Up to 5 days in refrigerator

PREP TIME: 5 min
COOK TIME: 15 min

1 tablespoon vegetable oil

1 (5- to 6-ounce) skinless salmon fillet, cut into 1-inch pieces

7 asparagus stalks, trimmed and cut into 1-inch pieces

Pinch salt

Pinch freshly ground black pepper

¼ cup cooking sake

THE NIGHT BEFORE

1. In a skillet, heat the vegetable oil over medium heat until it shimmers. Add the salmon and cook for 3 minutes, flipping it halfway through the cooking time.

2. Add the asparagus and season with salt and pepper.

3. Add the cooking sake and immediately cover the skillet. Turn the heat to low. Steam for 8 minutes.

4. Let cool before transferring to a clean container to refrigerate.

IN THE MORNING

Microwave half the salmon, covered, for 30 seconds, then transfer to a bento box.

Ingredient tip: If you buy frozen salmon, I recommend separating the frozen fillets and freezing them individually so they are easy to thaw when you need them.

Substitution tip: If you prefer not to use alcohol for cooking, use vegetable broth instead of sake.

Per serving: Calories: 221; Total fat: 13g; Sodium: 415mg; Cholesterol: 0mg; Total carbs: 3g; Fiber: 1g; Sugar: 1g; Protein: 21g

MUSHROOM PASTA BENTO

This is a very tasty, filling bento for vegetarians. It is eggless, meatless, and cheeseless—but I guarantee everybody will be satisfied. It has mushroom and basil penne pasta, flavorful baked herb tofu, and honey-glazed sweet potato. Although it doesn't seem like there is any Japanese food in this fusion bento, the recipes for the pasta and the sweet potato are based on popular Japanese dishes.

TIMING & PREP

Mushroom and Basil Penne Pasta (page 105): Make ahead (15 minutes) and freeze for up to 3 weeks.

Baked Herb Tofu (page 107): Make ahead (35 minutes) and refrigerate for up to 4 days.

Honey-Glazed Sweet Potato (page 108): Make ahead (20 minutes) and refrigerate for up to 3 days.

In the morning: Microwave the pasta, covered, for 2 to 3 minutes and put it in a bento box with the cold tofu and cold sweet potato.

Easy extra suggestions: celery, grape tomatoes, radishes, sliced cucumber

MUSHROOM AND BASIL PENNE PASTA

Freezing pasta dishes is quick and easy, especially when you make a large amount ahead of time and freeze it in individual servings. Moreover, frozen cooked penne is relatively insulated from drying out after reheating. Remember, however, that pasta dishes that have marinara or oil-based sauces are better suited for freezing. This recipe has sautéed mushrooms, basil, and a splash of soy sauce. It tastes amazing because the soy sauce complements the flavor of the sautéed mushrooms.

STORAGE: Up to 3 weeks in the freezer

PREP TIME: 5 min
COOK TIME: 10 min

Salt

8 ounces dried penne

3 tablespoons extra-virgin olive oil, divided

1 pound cremini mushrooms or any mushrooms you like, stemmed and sliced

1 tablespoon soy sauce

2 teaspoons dried basil

MAKE AHEAD

1. Fill a large pot with water and season it with salt. Bring it to a boil over high heat. Add the penne and cook according to the package directions until al dente.

2. Meanwhile, in a skillet, heat 1 tablespoon of olive oil over medium heat until it shimmers. Add the mushrooms and cook for 2 minutes. Season with salt and cook for 2 minutes more.

3. Drain the pasta and add it to the skillet. Stir in the soy sauce and the remaining 2 tablespoons of olive oil. Cook, stirring, for 1 minute. Sprinkle with the basil.

continued

4. Let cool. Divide the pasta into four portions, and transfer each portion to a clean container or zip-top bag to freeze.

IN THE MORNING

Microwave 1 serving of pasta, covered, for 2 to 3 minutes, stirring halfway through the cooking time.

Per serving: Calories: 318; Total fat: 11g; Sodium: 264mg; Cholesterol: 0mg; Total carbs: 45g; Fiber: 3g; Sugar: 1g; Protein: 11g

BAKED HERB TOFU

This dish offers a delicious, healthy protein in the form of tofu. The key to making tasty tofu is to season before draining it. The tofu will soak up all the seasoning while it drains because of the salt content of the seasoning. The seasoning is equal parts salt, onion powder, thyme, paprika, oregano, dill, and basil. Use any kind of herbs you want, but keep the percentage of salt (about 15 percent) unchanged. When the amount of salt is more or less, it makes the tofu either very salty or bland.

STORAGE: Up to 4 days in the refrigerator

PREP TIME: 25 min (including draining)
COOK TIME: 10 min

1 (14-ounce) package extra-firm tofu

1½ tablespoons Herb Seasoning (page 135)

1 tablespoon vegetable oil

THE NIGHT BEFORE

1. Drain the tofu and pat it dry with paper towels. Cut the tofu into ½-inch cubes.

2. Put the tofu cubes in a medium bowl and gradually sprinkle them with the herb seasoning while gently mixing to coat the tofu. Transfer the tofu to a plate lined with a paper towel, and cover with another paper towel. Let the tofu sit at room temperature for 15 to 20 minutes to drain.

3. In a skillet, heat the vegetable oil over medium heat until it shimmers. Put the tofu in the skillet and cook for 8 to 10 minutes, gently flipping the cubes every few minutes.

4. Let cool before transferring to a clean container to refrigerate.

IN THE MORNING

Put one-fourth of the cold tofu in a bento box.

Per serving: Calories: 128; Total fat: 10g; Sodium: 508mg; Cholesterol: 0mg; Total carbs: 3g; Fiber: 0g; Sugar: 1g; Protein: 10g

HONEY-GLAZED SWEET POTATO

This is a popular snack recipe called daigaku-imo in Japanese. The original recipe uses fried sweet potato, but here I will teach you a quick and easy nonfried version. It is healthier and tastes great! I also changed the traditional recipe slightly to accommodate American sweet potatoes, which have different water content than Japanese sweet potatoes.

STORAGE: Up to 3 days in the refrigerator

PREP TIME: 10 min
COOK TIME: 10 min

1 sweet potato, peeled and cut into 1-inch cubes

1 tablespoon butter or margarine

¼ cup honey

1 tablespoon sesame seeds, roasted

THE NIGHT BEFORE

1. Put the potato cubes on a microwave-safe plate and microwave for 3 to 4 minutes, covered, until tender.

2. In a skillet, melt the butter over medium-high heat. Add the sweet potato and cook for 3 minutes, stirring frequently, until slightly golden.

3. Add the honey and sesame seeds. Cook, spooning the glaze over the potatoes, for about 2 minutes.

4. Let cool before transferring to a clean container to refrigerate.

IN THE MORNING

Put half the cold glazed sweet potato in the bento box.

Cooking tip: To microwave the potato, put the smaller pieces in the middle of the plate and larger pieces toward the edge so it cooks evenly.

Per serving: Calories: 261; Total fat: 8g; Sodium: 104mg; Cholesterol: 0mg; Total carbs: 49g; Fiber: 3g; Sugar: 38g; Protein: 2g

CHINESE-INSPIRED BENTO

This bento does not use authentic Chinese foods, but, rather, Chinese-inspired foods: fried rice, miso-seasoned tofu, and sweet-and-sour eggplant. The taste is divine, and the texture is not greasy like American-Chinese food often is. A couple of these dishes may be new to you, but they are worth trying. I think you will discover this bento is one of your new favorites.

TIMING & PREP

Egg and Ham Fried Rice (page 110): Make in the morning (10 minutes) using one serving of frozen Steamed Rice (page 134).
Stir-Fried Tofu and Vegetables with Miso (page 111): Make ahead (20 minutes) and refrigerate for up to 4 days.
Sweet-and-Sour Eggplant and Bell Pepper (page 112): Make ahead (15 minutes) and refrigerate for up to 4 days.

In the morning: Microwave one serving of frozen Steamed Rice (page 134) for 2 to 3 minutes, then make the fried rice. Put the fried rice in a bento box with the cold tofu dish and cold eggplant.

Easy extra suggestions: celery, green grapes, kiwi (halved; bring a spoon), sliced cucumber

EGG AND HAM FRIED RICE

My mother sometimes cooked various kinds of fried rice for weekend brunch because it is easy, delicious, and healthy. It takes only 10 minutes if you have steamed rice to start with. Fried rice ingredients are very flexible, so use what you like or have in your refrigerator. My fried rice has rich flavor because I add consommé powder. I recommend making this dish in the morning with freshly cooked eggs, but it is also okay to make it the night before and keep it refrigerated.

STORAGE: 1 day in the refrigerator

PREP TIME: 5 min
COOK TIME: 5 min

1 serving frozen Steamed Rice (page 134)

1 tablespoon toasted sesame oil

1 large egg, beaten

1 thin slice turkey ham, chopped

½ teaspoon Ajinomoto consommé powder or other consommé powder you like

Freshly ground black pepper

Minced fresh parsley, for garnish

IN THE MORNING

1. Microwave the frozen rice, covered, for 2 to 3 minutes.

2. In a small skillet, heat the sesame oil over medium heat until it shimmers. Add the egg and heat until the edges are cooked. Add the rice and ham. Stir-fry for 3 minutes while crumbling the egg. Season with the consommé powder and pepper halfway through the cook time.

3. Transfer the fried rice to the bento box and sprinkle with the parsley.

Per serving: Calories: 533; Total fat: 21g; Sodium: 706mg; Cholesterol: 227mg; Total carbs: 61g; Fiber: 2g; Sugar: 1g; Protein: 21g

STIR-FRIED TOFU AND VEGETABLES WITH MISO

In Japan, a lot of dishes are stir-fried with miso sauce, so I always keep my homemade miso sauce handy in the refrigerator. Usually, tofu should be drained before cooking because of its high water content, which can make dishes bland. However, you don't need to drain the tofu for this recipe because it is crumbled and cooked to evaporate the water before seasoning.

STORAGE: Up to 4 days in the refrigerator

PREP TIME: 5 min
COOK TIME: 15 min

1 tablespoon toasted sesame oil

1 (14-ounce) package extra-firm tofu, drained

1 carrot, chopped

3 shiitake mushrooms or any mushrooms you like, stemmed and chopped

¼ cup Miso Sauce (page 139)

1 teaspoon Shimaya kombu dashi soup stock powder or any vegetable- or fish-based dashi powder

¼ teaspoon freshly ground black pepper

THE NIGHT BEFORE

1. In a skillet, heat the sesame oil over medium heat until it shimmers. Roughly crumble the tofu into the skillet and add the carrot and mushrooms. Stir-fry for 7 minutes or until the water from the tofu evaporates completely.

2. Add the miso sauce, dashi powder, and pepper. Cook, stirring, for 5 minutes more.

3. Let cool before transferring to a clean container to refrigerate.

IN THE MORNING

Transfer one-fourth of the cold tofu stir-fry to the bento box.

Cooking tip: This dish doesn't require that the tofu pieces be all the same size. It is fine if there are big and small chunks.

Per serving: Calories: 179; Total fat: 10g; Sodium: 736mg; Cholesterol: 0mg; Total carbs: 14g; Fiber: 2g; Sugar: 5g; Protein: 12g

SWEET-AND-SOUR EGGPLANT AND BELL PEPPER

Sweet-and-sour is a typical taste combination in Asian food. The seasonings used are vinegar, soy sauce, and sugar. In Japan, we have oppressively hot summer days and need energy to pull through, but the humidity makes us lose our appetite. In that situation, we eat vinegary dishes because vinegar helps increase appetite and digestion. For a beautiful presentation, I recommend using red and yellow bell peppers. To make the dish even tastier, remove the very center of the eggplant if it contains lots of seeds; the seeds give the eggplant a slightly bitter taste after storing.

STORAGE: Up to 4 days in the refrigerator

PREP TIME: 5 min
COOK TIME: 10 min

1 tablespoon toasted sesame oil

1 large eggplant, peeled and cut into 1-inch cubes

2 bell peppers, red and/or yellow, cored and cut into 1-inch squares

¼ cup soy sauce (gluten free if necessary)

1 tablespoon rice vinegar

1 tablespoon sugar

THE NIGHT BEFORE

1. In a skillet, heat the sesame oil over medium heat until it shimmers. Add the eggplant and bell peppers and cook for 5 minutes.

2. Add the soy sauce, vinegar, and sugar. Cook, stirring, for 5 minutes more.

3. Let cool before transferring to a clean container to refrigerate.

IN THE MORNING

Transfer one-fourth of the cold eggplant and bell pepper to the bento box.

Per serving: Calories: 99; Total fat: 4g; Sodium: 921mg; Cholesterol: 0mg; Total carbs: 15g; Fiber: 6g; Sugar: 9g; Protein: 3g

RICE OMELET BENTO

Kids love this bento, which features a rice omelet and sautéed potato with miso. Rice omelets are usually served on their own because they contain the perfect nutrient balance of good protein, carbs, and vitamins. But a one-dish bento seems boring, so we often add another dish (in this case sautéed vegetables), as well as some fruit. I recommend adding fruits or vegetables that are low in carbs and high in minerals.

TIMING & PREP

Rice Omelet (page 114): Cook in the morning (15 minutes) using one serving of frozen Steamed Rice (page 134).

Stir-Fried Potato and Green Bell Pepper with Miso (page 115): Make ahead (15 minutes) and refrigerate for up to 3 days.

In the morning: Microwave one serving of frozen Steamed Rice (page 134), covered, for 2 to 3 minutes. Make the omelet (15 minutes). Meanwhile, microwave the potato, covered, for 30 seconds. Combine the dishes in a bento box.

Easy extra suggestions: berries, cantaloupe, grape tomatoes, radishes, stick cheese

RICE OMELET

This is typical Japanese-style Western food, called omu-rice: fried rice seasoned with ketchup and covered with a thin fried egg crêpe. About a hundred years ago, a Japanese restaurant made this recipe as a meal for the restaurant's employees so they could be quickly nourished and get back to work. Nowadays, this is a favorite dish of Japanese kids because it is so delicious! Traditional omu-rice includes chicken or ham in the fried rice, but I use only onion so this dish is vegetarian. Add meat if you'd like.

PREP TIME: 5 min
COOK TIME: 10 min

1 serving frozen
Steamed Rice
(page 134)

2 tablespoons
vegetable oil, divided

¼ onion, chopped

¼ cup ketchup

Salt

Freshly ground
black pepper

2 large eggs, beaten

IN THE MORNING

1. Microwave the frozen rice, uncovered, for 2 to 3 minutes.

2. In a small skillet, heat 1 tablespoon of vegetable oil over medium heat until it shimmers. Add the onion and sauté for 2 minutes. Add the rice and ketchup and season with salt and pepper. Stir-fry for 3 minutes. Transfer to the bento box.

3. Wipe out the skillet with paper towels. Heat the remaining 1 tablespoon of vegetable oil over medium-low heat until it shimmers. Pour in the eggs and cook for 3 minutes, carefully flipping the omelet halfway through the cooking time. Place the egg on the rice in the bento box, and tuck in the edges.

Variation tip: Add any chopped vegetables and/or meat to the fried rice, such as broccoli, cabbage, carrot, corn, bacon, chicken, ham, and so on.

Per serving: Calories: 729; Total fat: 38g; Sodium: 966mg; Cholesterol: 372mg; Total carbs: 77g; Fiber: 3g; Sugar: 16g; Protein: 19g

STIR-FRIED POTATO AND GREEN BELL PEPPER WITH MISO

Potato, green bell pepper, and miso go really well together. Here, I use green bell pepper, but traditionally we use Japanese green pepper, which is thinner and has a softer texture and more bitter taste. The potato doesn't take long to cook because it is microwaved first.

STORAGE: Up to 3 days in the refrigerator

PREP TIME: 5 min
COOK TIME: 10 min

1 large russet potato, peeled and cut into ½-inch cubes

1 tablespoon toasted sesame oil

1 green bell pepper, cored and cut into ½-inch squares

3 tablespoons Miso Sauce (page 139)

THE NIGHT BEFORE

1. Put the potato cubes on a microwave-safe plate and microwave for 3 minutes, covered, until tender.

2. In a skillet, heat the sesame oil over medium heat until it shimmers. Add the potato and green bell pepper and cook for 6 minutes.

3. Add in the Miso Sauce and cook, stirring, for 1 minute, or until slightly brown.

4. Let cool before transferring to a clean container to refrigerate.

IN THE MORNING

Microwave one-third of the potato and green bell pepper, covered, for 30 seconds, then put it in the bento box.

Variation tip: Add any vegetables and/or meat you like, such as asparagus, eggplant, mushrooms, chicken, or fish.

Per serving: Calories: 195; Total fat: 6g; Sodium: 710mg; Cholesterol: 0mg; Total carbs: 33g; Fiber: 3g; Sugar: 7g; Protein: 5g

SWEET POTATO CROQUETTE BENTO

When I was a child, I was always so happy when my mother put a croquette in my bento! Her homemade croquettes were delicious. In Japanese culture, croquettes are often served with rice. I make this bento with edamame rice and sautéed mushrooms. It is a very delicious and nutritious vegetarian bento.

TIMING & PREP

Edamame Rice (page 117): Make ahead (75 minutes) and freeze for up to 3 weeks.

Cheesy Sweet Potato Croquettes (page 119): Make ahead (70 minutes) and freeze for up to 3 weeks.

Sautéed Mushrooms with Buttery Soy Sauce (page 121): Make ahead (15 minutes) and refrigerate for up to 2 days.

In the morning: Microwave the rice, covered, for 2 to 3 minutes. Microwave the croquettes, wrapped in paper towels, for 90 seconds. Then, microwave the mushroom for 30 seconds. Combine the dishes in a bento box.

Easy extra suggestions: berries, cantaloupe, grape tomatoes, hardboiled egg (halved) radishes, stick cheese

EDAMAME RICE

Edamame are young soybeans that are harvested before they have had the chance to mature. Edamame are lower in calories and higher in vitamins than mature soybeans. They have a light flavor and soft texture that everyone loves. Frozen shelled edamame are readily available nowadays, and modern freezing techniques ensure it retains its nutritional benefits.

 **STORAGE:** Up to 3 weeks in the freezer

PREP TIME: 40 min
COOK TIME: 35 min

1½ cups uncooked short-grain white rice

1⅔ cups water

1 teaspoon salt

1½ teaspoons cooking sake

½ cup frozen shelled edamame, rinsed to thaw

MAKE AHEAD

1. In a fine-mesh strainer set atop a bowl, rinse the rice under cool running water while stirring it with your hand. Drain the rice as soon as the water in the bowl turns a murky white color. Repeat until the water in the bowl is clear.

2. In a medium bowl, combine the rice and water; let soak for 30 minutes at room temperature.

3. Pour the rice with the soaking water into a deep saucepan and add the salt and cooking sake. Cover the pan and bring the mixture to a boil over high heat, about 5 minutes. Add the edamame and gently stir. Turn the heat to very low, cover the pan, and cook for 10 to 12 minutes. When there is no water left in the pan, turn the heat off, put a kitchen towel under the lid, and steam the rice and edamame for 10 minutes. This makes the rice softer. Stir carefully from the bottom of the pan.

continued

4. Divide the rice and edamame into four portions, and transfer each portion to a zip-top bag or glass container to freeze.

IN THE MORNING

Microwave one portion of the frozen rice, covered, for 2 to 3 minutes, and transfer to a bento box.

Cooking tip: Before putting a kitchen towel over the rice, check inside the pan. If there is still water in the pan, put the lid back on and cook for 2 more minutes, then check again. If you cook the rice in a rice cooker, add the edamame at the beginning because you cannot open the cooker while it is cooking.

Per serving: Calories: 281; Total fat: 1g; Sodium: 586mg; Cholesterol: 0mg; Total carbs: 61g; Fiber: 3g; Sugar: 0g; Protein: 6g

CHEESY SWEET POTATO CROQUETTES

Mixing shredded cheese and corn kernels into mashed sweet potato makes for a very cheesy, creamy, and tasty dish. The reason I use sweet potato is that it is high in vitamin C, potassium, and fiber. It also has a low glycemic index, which means that it doesn't make our blood sugar rise quickly, even though it does contain carbohydrates. Croquettes are great as a main dish and also for kids' snacks after school. Make a bunch ahead of time, and keep them on hand in the freezer.

STORAGE: Up to 3 weeks in the freezer

PREP TIME: 60 min
COOK TIME: 10 min

1 large sweet potato, peeled and cut into small pieces

1 teaspoon salt

½ teaspoon freshly ground black pepper

½ cup frozen sweet corn kernels, rinsed to thaw

½ cup shredded cheese, any type

Vegetable oil, for frying and greasing your hands

¼ cup all-purpose flour

1 large egg, beaten

1 cup bread crumbs

MAKE AHEAD

1. Put the sweet potato pieces on a microwave-safe plate and microwave, covered, for 3 to 4 minutes, until tender. Transfer to a medium bowl and add the salt and pepper. Mash the sweet potato. Refrigerate for 20 minutes.

2. Meanwhile, in a small bowl, combine the corn and cheese. Set aside.

3. Coat your hands with a bit of vegetable oil to keep the sweet potato from sticking to them. Divide the potato mixture into 8 portions, and spread one portion on your hand. Put about 1 tablespoon of the cheese filling in the center of the potato, then roll it up, shaping it into a cylinder about 2 inches long and 1 inch wide. Make sure there is no filling on the surface of the croquette. Repeat with the remaining sweet potato mixture and filling.

continued

4. Put the flour in a shallow bowl, the beaten egg in a second shallow bowl, and the bread crumbs in a third bowl. One at a time, roll the croquettes in the flour, dip them into the egg, and press them into the bread crumbs. Tap off any excess breading.

5. In a deep pan, heat 2 inches of vegetable oil over medium heat until it shimmers. Add 4 croquettes at a time and fry, flipping occasionally, until golden on all sides, about 5 minutes. Transfer to a wire rack to drain. Repeat with the remaining croquettes.

6. Once they are cool enough to handle, transfer the croquettes to a zip-top bag to freeze.

IN THE MORNING

Wrap 2 croquettes in paper towels and microwave for 90 seconds, turning them halfway through the cooking time. Put them in a bento box.

Cooking tip: To check whether the oil is hot enough to fry, drop some bread crumbs into it. If they float with bubbles, the oil is ready.

Safety tip: To fry the croquettes safely, use a deep pan that is at least twice the height of the amount of oil used. While frying, put a metal strainer upside-down, like a lid, on the skillet. This prevents oil from spattering everywhere.

Per serving: Calories: 257; Total fat: 14g; Sodium: 810mg; Cholesterol: 61mg; Total carbs: 25g; Fiber: 2g; Sugar: 3g; Protein: 9g

SAUTÉED MUSHROOMS WITH BUTTERY SOY SAUCE

Butter and soy sauce is a very common seasoning in Japan, as typified by butter-shoyu ramen soup and Japanese-style steak sauce. Moreover, you can find many kinds of Japanese snacks seasoned with butter and soy sauce, such as potato chips. The key to cooking this dish is to sauté the mushrooms over medium-high heat the whole time to allow the liquid they give off to evaporate, so the dish will keep longer and retain its flavor.

STORAGE: Up to 2 days in the refrigerator

PREP TIME: 5 min
COOK TIME: 10 min

1 tablespoon toasted sesame oil

1 pound mixed mushrooms (such as cremini, oyster, shiitake, and/or shimeji), stemmed and sliced

1 tablespoon butter or margarine

2 tablespoons soy sauce (gluten free if necessary)

3 tablespoons chopped scallion

THE NIGHT BEFORE

1. In a skillet, heat the sesame oil over medium-high heat until it shimmers. Add the mushrooms and sauté for 8 minutes. When there is 1 minute left, add the butter and soy sauce and stir to combine.

2. Let cool before transferring to a clean container to refrigerate.

IN THE MORNING

Microwave half the mushrooms for 30 seconds and put them in a bento box. Sprinkle with the scallion.

Storage tip: It is very handy to keep frozen chopped scallion in the freezer. You can use it without thawing. Wash the scallions first and dry them with paper towels. Finely chop the scallions and put them in a zip-top bag to freeze. Use within 3 weeks.

Per serving: Calories: 171; Total fat: 13g; Sodium: 983mg; Cholesterol: 0mg; Total carbs: 9g; Fiber: 3g; Sugar: 4g; Protein: 8g

CHICKEN MEATBALL BENTO

This bento contains a simple pasta dish with ham and cabbage, Japanese-style boiled chicken meatballs, and creamy potato salad with cucumber, all popular dishes in Japan. Because of the ingredients and the way the meatballs are boiled, the bento is filling but has a fresh, light taste. It has a good amount of protein and great carbs, so I recommend adding fruits that are high in vitamins to make the bento even healthier.

TIMING & PREP

Ham and Cabbage Spaghetti (page 123): Make ahead (15 minutes) and freeze for up to 3 weeks.

Japanese-Style Chicken Meatballs (page 124): Make ahead (20 minutes) and freeze for up to 3 weeks.

Creamy Potato Salad (page 125): Make ahead (15 minutes) and refrigerate for up to 3 days.

In the morning: Microwave the pasta, covered, for 2 to 3 minutes. Then, microwave the meatballs, covered, for 1 minute. Combine the pasta and meatballs with the cold potato salad in a bento box.

Easy extra suggestions: berries, cherries, grapes, kiwi (halved; bring a spoon), mandarin oranges

HAM AND CABBAGE SPAGHETTI

This is a very popular spring dish in Japan. Because ham is already salty, the only seasoning is pepper. Cabbage is high in calcium, potassium, and vitamins C, K, and U. Some stomach medicines contain vitamin U, because it restores the mucosa in our digestive tract. I often prepare this dish when I need a simple lunch.

STORAGE: Up to 3 weeks in the freezer

PREP TIME: 5 min
COOK TIME: 10 min

Salt

8 ounces dried spaghetti, broken in half

4 cabbage leaves, shredded

2 tablespoons olive oil, divided

4 thin slices turkey ham, cut into short strips

Pinch freshly ground black pepper

MAKE AHEAD

1. Fill a large saucepan with water, and season it with salt. Bring it to a boil over high heat, add the spaghetti, and cook for 8 to 10 minutes, stirring occasionally, until al dente. When there are 2 minutes left, add the cabbage to the pot. Drain the pasta and the cabbage together.

2. In a skillet, heat 1 tablespoon of olive oil over medium heat until it shimmers. Add the ham and cook for 1 minute. Add the pasta and cabbage to the skillet and drizzle with the remaining 1 tablespoon of olive oil. Season with the pepper and stir until the oil coats the pasta.

3. Let cool. Divide the pasta into four portions, and transfer each portion to a zip-top bag or glass container to freeze.

IN THE MORNING

Microwave one serving, covered, for 2 to 3 minutes, stirring halfway through the cooking time. Put the pasta in a bento box.

Per serving: Calories: 298; Total fat: 11g; Sodium: 691mg; Cholesterol: 82mg; Total carbs: 33g; Fiber: 1g; Sugar: 1g; Protein: 17g

JAPANESE-STYLE CHICKEN MEATBALLS

This is a traditional Japanese recipe called tori-dango. These meatballs have a juicy texture and a lovely, gingery flavor. They are often added to soups, hot pots, stir-fries, and so on. If you keep some in the freezer, you can add one more dish to your meal in less than 5 minutes. Moreover, the meatballs are boiled and made with chicken, so they are low in calories and fat.

STORAGE: Up to 3 weeks in the freezer

PREP TIME: 5 min
COOK TIME: 15 min

1 pound ground chicken

2 teaspoons soy sauce (gluten free if necessary)

3 tablespoons cornstarch

2 tablespoons chopped scallion

1 teaspoon grated peeled fresh ginger

1 teaspoon salt

MAKE AHEAD

1. Bring a large pot of water to a boil over high heat, then turn the heat down to medium.

2. Meanwhile, in a large bowl, combine the ground chicken, soy sauce, cornstarch, scallion, ginger, and salt. Mix well for at least 2 minutes. Using two spoons, shape the chicken mixture into balls slightly smaller than golf balls.

3. Drop half the meatballs into the boiling water and cook until they float, about 6 minutes. Use a slotted spoon to transfer the meatballs to paper towels to drain. Repeat with the remaining meatballs.

4. Once cool, transfer the meatballs to a zip-top bag to freeze.

IN THE MORNING

Microwave 3 or 4 meatballs, covered, for 1 minute and put them in a bento box.

Per serving (3 meatballs): Calories: 124; Total fat: 6g; Sodium: 533mg; Cholesterol: 64mg; Total carbs: 4g; Fiber: 0g; Sugar: 0g; Protein: 13g

CREAMY POTATO SALAD

The ingredients in this simple recipe are potato, cucumber, and mayonnaise. For bento safety, I cook the potato in the microwave instead of boiling it and salt the sliced cucumber to reduce the water content. Though some people avoid potatoes or mayonnaise (due to carbs or calorie concerns), I believe that these foods can be part of a healthy diet if consumed in moderation.

STORAGE: Up to 3 days in the refrigerator

PREP TIME: 12 min
COOK TIME: 3 min

1 baby cucumber, thinly sliced

¼ teaspoon salt

2 small russet potatoes, peeled and cut into chunks

¼ cup mayonnaise

Freshly ground black pepper

THE NIGHT BEFORE

1. In a small bowl, combine the cucumber and salt. Let sit for about 3 minutes at room temperature. Rinse the cucumber under running water and wring it dry by hand.

2. Meanwhile, put the potato chunks on a microwave-safe plate and microwave for 2 to 3 minutes, until tender. Transfer to a medium bowl and mash with a fork.

3. Stir in the mayonnaise and cucumber, and season with pepper. Transfer to a clean container to refrigerate.

IN THE MORNING

Put one-third of the cold potato salad in the bento box.

Cooking tip: When microwaving the potato, place small chunks in the center of the plate and larger chunks toward the edge so they cook evenly.

Variation tip: Add any seasonings you choose, such as basil, onion powder, or red pepper flakes.

Per serving: Calories: 206; Total fat: 14g; Sodium: 322mg; Cholesterol: 7mg; Total carbs: 20g; Fiber: 3g; Sugar: 2g; Protein: 2g

NAPOLITAN SPAGHETTI BENTO

This Italian-Japanese fusion bento has recently become common in Japan. It contains Napolitan spaghetti (a dish created by a Japanese chef inspired by an American chef), turkey burgers, and dashi-flavored egg. Most people in Japan eat egg in their bento every day. Add fruits or veggies high in vitamin C to this bento, because the vegetables in the pasta lose a bit of their nutritional value when cooked and, although egg has valuable nutrients, it does not contain vitamin C.

TIMING & PREP

Napolitan Spaghetti (page 127): Make ahead (20 minutes) and freeze for up to 3 weeks.

Turkey Burgers (page 129): Make ahead (45 minutes) and freeze for up to 3 weeks.

Japanese Dashi-Flavored Fried Egg (page 131): Cook in the morning (5 minutes).

In the morning: Microwave the pasta, covered, for 2 to 3 minutes. Microwave the turkey burgers, covered, for 2 minutes. Meanwhile, make the fried egg. Combine the dishes in a bento box.

Easy extra suggestions: cherries, kiwi (halved; bring a spoon), oranges, strawberries

NAPOLITAN SPAGHETTI

This is a popular dish created by a Japanese chef around 1945. Before World War II, there were authentic Italian tomato pasta recipes in Japan, but the war brought a food shortage, making tomatoes hard to get. When Japan was under U.S. control, a hotel chef was inspired by a dish of spaghetti with ketchup he saw an American soldier eat, so he put it on the restaurant's menu. The dish is clearly not authentic Italian—the pasta is cooked tender rather than al dente and ketchup is certainly not an Italian sauce—but people still like it because it has become part of Japanese cuisine over the years. If you go to Japan, you will find this delicious pasta everywhere.

STORAGE: Up to 3 weeks in the freezer

PREP TIME: 5 min
COOK TIME: 15 min

Salt

8 ounces spaghetti, broken in half

1 tablespoon vegetable oil

½ onion, sliced

½ green bell pepper, thinly sliced

3 thin slices turkey ham, cut into thin strips

½ cup ketchup

Freshly ground black pepper

Grated Parmesan cheese, for garnish

MAKE AHEAD

1. Fill a large pot with water and season it with salt. Bring it to a boil over high heat. Add the pasta and cook for about 10 minutes, until very tender. Drain.

2. Meanwhile, in a skillet, heat the vegetable oil over medium heat until it shimmers. Add the onion, bell pepper, and ham and cook for 3 minutes.

3. Add the drained pasta and ketchup to the skillet. Stir-fry for 3 minutes, until slightly browned, seasoning with pepper halfway through the cooking time.

4. Let cool. Divide the pasta into four portions, and transfer each portion to a zip-top bag or glass container to freeze.

continued

NAPOLITAN SPAGHETTI continued

IN THE MORNING

Microwave one serving of pasta, covered, for 2 to 3 minutes, stirring halfway through the cooking time. Put the pasta in a bento box and sprinkle with Parmesan cheese.

Cleanup tip: To keep the sauce from staining the bento box, rinse the bento box with running water as soon as possible after eating, then wipe the inside dry.

Per serving: Calories: 347; Total fat: 7g; Sodium: 886mg; Cholesterol: 33mg; Total carbs: 54g; Fiber: 3g; Sugar: 10g; Protein: 17g

TURKEY BURGERS

Japan has a big hamburger culture. We often cook them at home, and we have many hamburger restaurants. Japanese hamburgers are served without a bun, in the style of a German steak dish. In Japan, a mixture of ground beef and pork is often used, but I use ground turkey in this recipe. You can use any kind of meat and mix in any kind of chopped vegetables you like, such as broccoli, cabbage, carrots, and mushrooms. Sometimes Japanese people add crumbled tofu.

STORAGE: Up to 3 weeks in the freezer

PREP TIME: 15 min
COOK TIME: 30 min

1 pound ground turkey

1 small onion, finely chopped

1 large egg, beaten

½ cup bread crumbs

1 heaping teaspoon salt

¼ teaspoon freshly ground black pepper

1 tablespoon vegetable oil

MAKE AHEAD

1. In a medium bowl, mix together the ground turkey, onion, egg, bread crumbs, salt, and pepper. Shape the turkey mixture into 10 palm-size balls, and flatten them with your hands into patties.

2. In a large skillet, heat the vegetable oil over medium heat until it shimmers. Add half of the burgers and cook for 3 minutes, then flip them. Cover the skillet, turn the heat to low, and cook for 7 minutes more. Transfer to paper towels to drain. Repeat with the remaining burgers.

3. Let cool before transferring to a zip-top bag to freeze.

continued

IN THE MORNING

Microwave 1 or 2 burgers, covered, for 2 minutes, flipping them halfway through the cooking time. Put the burgers in a bento box.

Safety tip: To ensure that the meat is cooked through, make holes on the surface using a toothpick and check to see that the juices run clear. If it is undercooked, cook for a few more minutes over low heat with the cover on until the juices run clear. If possible, bring the bento box with an ice pack in a cooler bag, and keep it away from warm places. Or store the bento in a refrigerator, if one is available.

Per serving (1 burger): Calories: 101; Total fat: 5g; Sodium: 279mg; Cholesterol: 19mg; Total carbs: 5g; Fiber: 0g; Sugar: 1g; Protein: 11g

JAPANESE DASHI-FLAVORED FRIED EGG

This is the best egg dish I have ever had. I never get tired of the taste—even if I eat it every day. Interestingly, fried eggs are seasoned in different ways in west and east Japan. In western Japan, the taste is savory, seasoned with soy sauce and dashi powder, which is the flavor I introduce you to here. In eastern Japan, it has a slightly sweet taste because sugar is added. Try my Microwaved Fried Egg (page 40) to compare. I grew up in Osaka, which is in western Japan, so this is my soul food.

PREP TIME: 2 min
COOK TIME: 3 min

1 tablespoon vegetable oil

2 large eggs

½ teaspoon soy sauce (gluten free if necessary)

¼ teaspoon Ajinomoto hondashi bonito soup stock, or any dashi powder you like

IN THE MORNING

1. In a skillet, heat the vegetable oil over medium heat until it shimmers.

2. In a small bowl, whisk together the eggs, soy sauce, and dashi powder. Pour the egg mixture into the skillet. Turn the heat to low and cook for 30 to 60 seconds, until the color of the egg's surface changes to light yellow. Flip the eggs and cook the other side until firm and cooked through. Fold the egg in half, and again if needed, to fit into the bento box.

Per serving: Calories: 268; Total fat: 24g; Sodium: 289mg; Cholesterol: 372mg; Total carbs: 1g; Fiber: 0g; Sugar: 1g; Protein: 13g

SESAME DRESSING PAGE 137

STAPLES & SAUCES

The recipes in this chapter are essential for many of the dishes in this book. These are things I can't live without! They are quick, easy staples and sauces that can be stored for a long time, and they make your bento preparation and cooking a lot easier—and tastier.

When you make a sauce in advance with a variety of ingredients such as those in this chapter, you ultimately use less of the individual sauce ingredients than if you added these ingredients to your food directly. This helps reduce sugar and salt intake.

Using store-bought sauces may be easier, but they contain a lot of sugar, salt, and chemical preservatives, which can have negative affects on your health.

If you follow a gluten-free diet, make sure to use gluten-free soy sauce.

STEAMED RICE

Steamed rice is a staple food in Japanese cuisine. For people without rice cookers, it is essential to learn how to cook rice on the stovetop—and it is easier than you might think. In fact, many people think pan-cooked rice is tastier than rice made in a rice cooker.

STORAGE: Up to 3 weeks in the freezer

PREP TIME: 40 min
COOK TIME: 35 min

1½ cups uncooked short-grain white rice

1⅔ cups water

1 teaspoon rice vinegar

1. In a fine-mesh strainer set atop a bowl, rinse the rice under cool running water while stirring it with your hand. Drain the rice as soon as the water in the bowl turns a murky white color. Repeat until the water in the bowl is clear.

2. In a medium bowl, combine the rice and water; let soak for 30 minutes at room temperature.

3. Pour the rice and the soaking water into a deep saucepan. Cover the pan and bring the mixture to a boil over high heat, about 5 minutes. Turn the heat to very low and cook for 10 to 12 minutes. When there is no water left in the pan, turn off the heat, put a kitchen towel under the lid, and steam the rice for 10 minutes. This makes the rice softer.

4. Add the vinegar and carefully stir from the bottom of the pan to combine. The vinegar helps the rice stay fresh in the bento box.

5. Divide the rice into four portions and put each portion into a zip-top bag or glass container to freeze.

Per serving: Calories: 269; Total fat: 0g; Sodium: 1mg; Cholesterol: 0mg; Total carbs: 59g; Fiber: 2g; Sugar: 0g; Protein: 5g

HERB SEASONING

I created this seasoning when I was trying to recreate the taste of tofu in a salad I ate at a restaurant when visiting New Jersey. I experimented many times to get the right flavor. This recipe is not exactly the same as the one I had at the restaurant—I think it is even more delicious! It can be used to season omelets, sautéed vegetables, grilled fish, and grilled meat. Shake well before using, as the ingredients separate during storage.

STORAGE: Up to 1 month in the refrigerator

PREP TIME: 3 min

1 teaspoon salt

1 teaspoon onion powder

1 teaspoon paprika

1 teaspoon dried oregano

1 teaspoon dried basil

1 teaspoon dried thyme

1 teaspoon dried dill

Rinse a small glass jar and lid with hot water to sterilize, then dry it thoroughly. Combine the salt, onion powder, paprika, oregano, basil, thyme, and dill in the jar. Cover and keep refrigerated. Shake before each use.

Per serving: Calories: 24; Total fat: 1g; Sodium: 2330mg; Cholesterol: 0mg; Total carbs: 5g; Fiber: 2g; Sugar: 1g; Protein: 1g

VERSATILE SAUCE

The combination of soy sauce, cooking sake, mirin, and sugar forms an essential sauce for Japanese cuisine. It is perfect in teriyaki dishes and many others. To give dishes varied flavors, I sometimes add extra cooking sake or mirin to this sauce while it's cooking.

STORAGE: Up to 1 month in the refrigerator

PREP TIME: 3 min
COOK TIME: 30 seconds

¼ cup soy sauce (gluten free if necessary)

¼ cup mirin

2 tablespoons cooking sake

1 tablespoon sugar

1. Rinse an 8-ounce glass jar and lid with hot water to sterilize. Combine the soy sauce, mirin, cooking sake, and sugar in the jar, and stir well.

2. Microwave for 30 seconds to melt the sugar. Mix well. Cover and keep refrigerated.

Per serving (¼ cup): Calories: 198; Total fat: 0g; Sodium: 4114mg; Cholesterol: 0mg; Total carbs: 46g; Fiber: 0g; Sugar: 30g; Protein: 4g

SESAME DRESSING

In Japanese cooking, it is good to have five tastes—sweet, sour, salty, spicy, and bitter—in a meal. To enjoy bitter vegetables, such as aralia sprouts, mustard greens, and bitter melon, Japanese cooks use this delicious, sweet dressing. Nowadays, the dressing is used on a variety of vegetables, such as asparagus, carrot, okra, spinach, and squash.

STORAGE: Up to 1 month in the refrigerator

PREP TIME: 3 min

6 tablespoons sesame seeds, roasted and ground

3 tablespoons sugar

3 tablespoons soy sauce (gluten free if necessary)

3 tablespoons mirin

Rinse an 8-ounce glass jar and lid with hot water to sterilize. Combine the ground sesame seeds, sugar, soy sauce, and mirin in the jar, and stir until the sugar dissolves. Cover and keep refrigerated.

Per serving (2 tablespoons): Calories: 136; Total fat: 7g; Sodium: 775mg; Cholesterol: 0mg; Total carbs: 18g; Fiber: 2g; Sugar: 12g; Protein: 3g

PICKLING LIQUID

This liquid has a refreshing taste and nutty sesame flavor. It is not only good for pickling vegetables but also makes a nice sauce for dim sum and plain fried rice. For those dishes, add a touch of freshly squeezed lemon or lime juice along with the pickling liquid.

STORAGE: Up to 3 weeks in the refrigerator

PREP TIME: 3 min

½ cup toasted sesame oil

¼ cup soy sauce (gluten free if necessary)

¼ cup rice vinegar

Rinse an 8-ounce glass jar and lid with hot water to sterilize. Combine the sesame oil, soy sauce, and vinegar in the jar. Cover and keep refrigerated.

Per serving (1 tablespoon): Calories: 65; Total fat: 7g; Sodium: 224mg; Cholesterol: 0mg; Total carbs: 0g; Fiber: 0g; Sugar: 0g; Protein: 0g

MISO SAUCE

I use this delicious sauce for many types of dishes, such as sautéed, grilled, and simmered vegetables and meat. I also love it for fish-based hot pot dishes. You can also use the sauce as a marinade for fish, meat, and vegetables. Miso is a very healthy fermented ingredient that is also high in vitamins, minerals, and protein. Every time I need more nutrients in a meal, I add this sauce to one or more of the components.

STORAGE: Up to 3 weeks in the refrigerator

PREP TIME: 3 min

3 tablespoons mixed (awase) miso

1 tablespoon soy sauce (gluten free if necessary)

1 tablespoon cooking sake

1 tablespoon mirin

1½ teaspoons sugar

Rinse a small glass jar and lid with hot water to sterilize. Combine the miso, soy sauce, cooking sake, mirin, and sugar in the jar, and stir until the sugar dissolves. Cover and keep refrigerated.

Per serving (1 tablespoon): Calories: 46; Total fat: 1g; Sodium: 797mg; Cholesterol: 0mg; Total carbs: 8g; Fiber: 1g; Sugar: 4g; Protein: 2g

MEASUREMENT CONVERSIONS

	US STANDARD	US STANDARD (OUNCES)	METRIC (APPROXIMATE)
VOLUME EQUIVALENTS (LIQUID)	2 tablespoons	1 fl. oz.	30 mL
	¼ cup	2 fl. oz.	60 mL
	½ cup	4 fl. oz.	120 mL
	1 cup	8 fl. oz.	240 mL
	1½ cups	12 fl. oz.	355 mL
	2 cups or 1 pint	16 fl. oz.	475 mL
	4 cups or 1 quart	32 fl. oz.	1 L
	1 gallon	128 fl. oz.	4 L
VOLUME EQUIVALENTS (DRY)	⅛ teaspoon	————	0.5 mL
	¼ teaspoon	————	1 mL
	½ teaspoon	————	2 mL
	¾ teaspoon	————	4 mL
	1 teaspoon	————	5 mL
	1 tablespoon	————	15 mL
	¼ cup	————	59 mL
	⅓ cup	————	79 mL
	½ cup	————	118 mL
	⅔ cup	————	156 mL
	¾ cup	————	177 mL
	1 cup	————	235 mL
	2 cups or 1 pint	————	475 mL
	3 cups	————	700 mL
	4 cups or 1 quart	————	1 L
	½ gallon	————	2 L
	1 gallon	————	4 L
WEIGHT EQUIVALENTS	½ ounce	————	15 g
	1 ounce	————	30 g
	2 ounces	————	60 g
	4 ounces	————	115 g
	8 ounces	————	225 g
	12 ounces	————	340 g
	16 ounces or 1 pound	————	455 g

	FAHRENHEIT (F)	CELSIUS (C) (APPROXIMATE)
OVEN TEMPERATURES	250°F	120°C
	300°F	150°C
	325°F	180°C
	375°F	190°C
	400°F	200°C
	425°F	220°C
	450°F	230°C

RESOURCES

Japanese Ordinary Bento. musubibento.wordpress.com

Kurihara, Harumi. *Everyday Harumi: Simple Japanese Food for Family and Friends* (London: Octopus Publishing Group, 2009).

NHK World—Japan. "Dining with the Chef: Japanese Food." www.nhk.or.jp /dwc/food.

Tsuyoshi, Tsuduki. "The '1975 Diet' and the Secret of Japanese Longevity" (June 6, 2019). www.nippon.com/en/in-depth/d00482/the-1975-diet -and-the-secret-of-japanese-longevity.html.

INDEX

ACKNOWLEDGMENTS

A special thank you to my mother, who passed away when I was 20 years old. I appreciate that she taught me many things and led me in the direction that is best for me. She is the inspiration that drove me to write my blog and this book, and she is the source of many recipes here. I wish she could read this book. I miss you so much, Mom.

Thank you to my husband, Frank, for your endless love and support—even when you are super busy. You always reassure me, and your experience as a law professor, with publishers, and writing your own books, was invaluable while I was writing this book. Moreover, I really appreciate your funny jokes that always calm me when I am stressed.

Thank you to my grandmother, who is 95 years old and still lives by herself. She taught me how to cut up a whole fish, which my grandfather caught each day. Her favorite phrase is, "If the dish is bland, add seasoning. If the dish has too strong a taste, cook it with more water. That's it!" She inspired me to recognize that cooking need not be difficult.

ABOUT THE AUTHOR

Chika Ravitch grew up near Osaka, Japan, and, after moving to the United States, created Japanese-food.org to share her tips on making traditional, healthy Japanese food using familiar ingredients. Chika earned a degree in analytical chemistry and wrote her senior thesis on the effects of lithium on the human body and mental health. From there, she began working for Japanese cosmetics company VECUA. She was an area manager overseeing five shops throughout the Kansai region and was able to learn a lot about business management and the benefits of Japanese approaches to healthy living.

As an executive at VECUA, she received special training each month on nutrition, skin biology, the effect of cosmetic ingredients on skin, and human biology. When she moved to the Midwest with her husband, Frank, she decided to use her knowledge to teach people about Japanese nutrition and cooking, and how to make traditional homemade Japanese dishes that are both healthy and delicious—all of which led to the creation of Japanese-food.org.

CPSIA information can be obtained
at www.ICGtesting.com
Printed in the USA
BVHW061525030120
568396BV00003B/3

9 781646 111350